We with Our Children

We with Our Children

A Commentary on the Form for Baptism

by
Cornelis Harinck

REFORMATION HERITAGE BOOKS
Grand Rapids, Michigan

REFORMATION HERITAGE BOOKS
2965 Leonard St., NE
Grand Rapids, MI 49525
616-977-0599 / Fax 616-285-3246
e-mail: orders@heritagebooks.org
website: www.heritagebooks.org

10 digit ISBN #1-892777-92-4
13 digit ISBN #978-1-892777-92-8

For additional Reformed literature, both new and used, request a free book list from Reformation Heritage Books at the above address.

Table of Contents

Preface

With great pleasure, I write this brief preface to *We with Our Children* by Rev. Cor Harinck, a prolific author and now retired minister in the Gereformeerde Gemeenten in the Netherlands. Rev. Harinck served six congregations (five in the Netherlands, and one in America, in Franklin Lakes, New Jersey, 1971-1974) over a span of forty-one years of active ministry. During the early 1970s, Rev. Harinck's clear, Reformed, and liberating preaching was a healing tonic for many souls, including mine. Under his ministry, I was first drawn to the Lord's Supper in Franklin Lakes; here, too, he befriended me with wise, loving, pastoral counsel, and has continued to serve as a spiritual mentor and dear friend to me for thirty-five years.

We with Our Children provides an enlightening, balanced, and detailed exposition of the Dutch Reformed "Form for the Administration of Baptism." It guides us through all the potential landmines associated with baptism and provides us with a rich, edifying treatment of infant baptism. Every office-bearer and parent should read this book.

Heartfelt thanks is owed to Jaap Evers, from New Zealand, for his translation from the Dutch language, and to Kate DeVries who greatly assisted me in editing it and readying it for print. May God richly bless this volume in English (as He has done in Dutch) to foster a greater understanding of the proper value and preciousness of the sacrament of baptism.

—Joel R. Beeke

CHAPTER 1

The Doctrine of Baptism in General

In this book, we will consider the form of baptism and show the authors' intent in order to fully understand its deep content. Here beats the heart of the Reformation; here we truly arrive at the roots of the Reformation.

First we shall consider the heading: "Form for the Administration of Baptism to Infants of Believers." This translation deviates from the original version. Originally, it read, "Form for the Administration of Holy Baptism." The revisionists at the national Synod at Dordrecht titled it the "Form for the Administration of Baptism to Children," so that in their report they could distinguish it from the form for the administration of baptism to adults. The publishers later added the words "to infants of believers." Thus, according to its original, the heading should really be "Form for the Administration of Holy Baptism," to which might be added "to children."

Children of Wrath

The principal parts of the doctrine of holy baptism are these three: First. That we with our children are conceived and born in sin, and therefore are children of wrath, insomuch that we cannot enter into the kingdom of God, except we are born again. This, the dipping in, or sprinkling with water teaches us, whereby the impurity of our souls is signified, and we admonished to loathe and humble ourselves before God, and seek for our purification and salvation without ourselves.

The form for the administration of baptism starts with a very honest confession of man's misery. We, with our children, are conceived and born in sin. This confession of man's total depravity should be reason for deep humility. We are born already depraved. The tender child brought to baptism has been born defiled by heritage. From the hour of birth, he is covered with the filth of sin and is offensive before God's holy eyes. This made David cry out, "Behold, I was shapen in iniquity; and in sin did my mother conceive me" (Ps. 51:5).

However, we should also note the connection that is made here between children and parents. The form says, "we with our children." The children received this sinful nature from their parents. When we look into the cradle of our children, we should not only allow this awful truth to penetrate our minds—that the child has been conceived and born in sin—but also acknowledge the relationship between the children and us. Our children inherit the sinful nature from us. This is the first element of the doctrine of baptism. It associates parents and children, and the form returns to this repeatedly. The covenant of grace concerns us and our children. Many boast of the fact that God propagates His grace through generations, and indeed, this is the doctrine of the covenant of grace. According to His unspeakable faithfulness, God works in the generations of those who keep His covenant and Word.

But first there is the message that we with our children are conceived and born in sin, after which follows the message of the covenant of grace. It is superficial and misleading to only say, "We with our children are covenant children and heirs of the promises of God." This ignores the fact that we are all conceived and born in sin and are children of wrath who can come into the kingdom of God only by regenerating grace. I fear that many who say that they are children of the covenant have not yet experienced that they are children of wrath. Behind the relationship of parents and children, there is first an association with guilt. And what a large amount of guilt is hidden behind this! Here the terrible reality of our fall is preached to us. The moment we departed from God, we, as children of Adam, brought forth children in our image and after our likeness and no longer in God's image and after God's likeness. Although our newborn children do not commit sin by their actions, they have the seed of sin in their hearts and therefore they are condemnable before God. Here we have a reason for each parent to deeply humble himself and to cry out with Job, "Who can bring a clean thing out of an unclean? not one" (Job 14:4). As a consequence of this hereditary sin, the root of all evil lies in the heart of the newly born child, who carries within himself the seed of the most filthy and base sins.

This is different from what is heard everywhere these days. The old confession of being conceived and born in sin is rejected and, in contrast, a good origin is professed to be present in man. This good mindset just has to be developed, it is said, and a different generation will inhabit the earth. Oh, what foolishness! For 6,000 years already, man has tried to better himself and the result is that the world is more and more corrupt. It would be better if Scripture, with its divine authority, would rule our opinions. Let us deeply humble ourselves under the confession that "we with our children are conceived and born in sin and therefore are children of wrath." In Ephesians 2:3 the apostle says, "...and were by nature the children of wrath, even as others." We are born under a dark cloud of wrath and we progress that way through life. If, between the cradle and the grave, we do not shelter in Him who has borne the wrath of God against sin, then that wrath shall rest upon us eternally.

Who can fathom the misery into which sin has brought us? We *are* children of wrath. It does not say that we *become* children of wrath when we die unconverted. No, we are children of wrath, even from the hour of our conception. We do not go lost, but we are lost. Man is born wretched!

But why does the author of the form emphasize this so much? Why do we need to hear the same message again and again, also in sermons? It is necessary because the authors want to speak of the divine mercy exhibited in baptism, and that mercy can only be spoken of rightly when there is someone who needs that mercy. This makes the wonder even greater—that a triune God has worked out salvation for a part of the deeply fallen race of Adam.

We are children of wrath "insomuch that we cannot enter into the kingdom of God, except we are born again." From the moment Adam sinned, the door of admission into God's presence was bolted. God was so terribly angry at the rebellion of man that He drove him out of the Garden of Eden and placed cherubim to guard the path to the tree of life.

By nature, there is no access for us to the kingdom of God—that is, to the renewed kingdom of God's grace. Not only were we driven out of Paradise and from heaven, but we were driven out of the kingdom of God. We cannot enter that kingdom, which one day will be unfolded in such glory, the way we are born. There is only one way to enter into that kingdom—namely, we must be born again.

The solemn word of Jesus to Nicodemus is heard: "Verily, verily, I say unto thee, Except a man be born again, he cannot see the kingdom of God" (John 3:3). An entirely new birth is what we need. We have to be recreated and born into that new kingdom of God if we are to have a part in it; there is no other way for a child of wrath to enter it. Here the author touches the heart of baptism. Just as the Holy Supper is the sacrament of continual nourishment, holy baptism is the sacrament of the new birth and engrafting into Christ. Holy baptism represents renewal of life. The water of baptism preaches to us of the new birth. Our first birth is in sin, and therefore we need to be born again. There is no stronger condemnation of our whole life; it cannot be improved upon, and we need to be born again. A wonder greater than the creation of the world itself must happen to man: a new spiritual birth. This doctrine is the doctrine of holy baptism. This is all visibly taught and shown to us.

The form for the administration of baptism continues thus: "This, the dipping in, or sprinkling with water teaches us, whereby the impurity of our souls is signified...."

Baptism contains visible divine instruction. The person is immersed in or sprinkled with the water. Thus, man requires cleansing. He requires immersion in or sprinkling with water. Water washes away the bodily uncleanness. Likewise, we have to be cleansed from sin through the blood of Christ.

This picture was abundantly clear to the Middle Eastern person whose feet became dirty because of so much dust and consequently had to be washed every time he entered a house. Every good host welcomed his guests at the door of his home with water to wash their feet.

Thus, the water of baptism testifies, "Because you are unclean, you must be washed." This is not only visibly preached with immersion, but also with sprinkling, although immersion more clearly demonstrates it, as the person goes totally under water. Yet, the same thing is portrayed with sprinkling because the countenance is the mirror of the soul. With that in mind, Christ said, "But if thine eye be evil, thy whole body shall be full of darkness." What a message those drops of water on the infant's forehead speak to us! They cry out, "Unclean, unclean!" Baptism, whether by immersion or by sprinkling, signifies being buried in the death of Christ. The sinner must be washed in the blood of Christ. Sin is filth from two points of view: as guilt and as blemish. Everything, therefore, bears the mark of uncleanness. Sin has made us so unclean that we need to be washed. "This, the dipping in, or sprinkling with water teaches us, so that we are admonished to loathe and humble ourselves before God, and seek for our purification and salvation without ourselves." The purpose of the visual instruction in baptism is delineated for us. Baptism admonishes us to:

• loathe ourselves;
• humble ourselves before God;
• seek purification and salvation without ourselves.

"To loathe ourselves." This is to abhor ourselves because of sin. The sinner pronounces a condemning judgment of himself and cries out with Asaph, "I was as a beast before thee" (Ps. 73:22). With the publican, he stands afar off and is so ashamed of his sins that he does not dare to lift up his face unto heaven. Although we by nature love ourselves, the revelation of sin teaches us to loathe ourselves and to be ashamed before God. Furthermore, we need "to humble ourselves before God." By nature we blame circumstances, and amid all our confessing that we are sinners we remain exalted and proud. True self-knowledge, however, humbles us before God. The heart is turned. This made Job bow deeply before God and say, "I have heard of thee by the hearing of the ear: but now mine eye seeth thee. Wherefore I abhor myself, and repent in dust and ashes" (Job 42:5-6). The soul is humbled, unworthy, and without rights; it says:

> *Against Thee only have I sinned,*
> *Done evil in Thy sight;*
> *Lord, in Thy judgment Thou art just,*
> *And in Thy sentence right.*

A true knowledge of sin works an upright penitence. Such a person cannot bow deeply enough before God because of shame and self-abhorrence. We will "seek for our purification and salvation without ourselves." We are inclined to look for all this within ourselves or by ourselves. Baptism admonishes us to seek this outside of ourselves. The water of baptism so clearly shows our total uncleanness; only help from outside us can save us. The water of baptism points pictorially to this help from without when the infant is cleansed by water, which is a cleansing agent outside the child. The form does not speak clearly about this here, but the water of baptism admonishes us now to seek for our purification and salvation outside of ourselves after having shown us our total uncleanness.

Where will we find cleansing and purification from sin? It will never be found in ourselves. Only in Christ's blood can that purification be found. The knowledge of our total sinfulness teaches us to seek for salvation in Christ.

Man will not seek his salvation outside of himself until and unless he has understood the language of the water of baptism, which has declared him to be totally unclean. Total depravity and the inability to ever change himself drive the sinner to seek purification and salvation outside of himself. All our seeking within ourselves is proof that we have never understood the preaching of the water of baptism regarding our total depravity and misery. A total uncleanness causes a holy despair regarding all that is of ourselves. All our righteousness becomes as filthy rags and the search for purification and salvation outside of ourselves is born.

Our fathers confessed this so beautifully in the original, unabridged form for the administration of baptism prior to 1574 when they said, "It admonishes us to humble ourselves before God and to loathe ourselves; thus to prepare ourselves to desire His grace, so that therewith all the wickedness and depravity of our old nature be washed away and buried, because we cannot be partakers of God's grace unless all our prior relying on our own capability, wisdom, and righteousness be removed from our hearts—until we wholly condemn all that is in us." This powerfully emphasizes the necessity of totally looking away from ourselves and seeking our purification and salvation outside of ourselves.

The water of baptism teaches us all these things. When we bring our children into the church to be washed with water (a sign of Jesus' blood) as commanded by Christ, what else do we testify except that they are unclean? Yes, even so unclean that nothing but Jesus' blood and Spirit can cleanse them. And when we have them baptized by the minister in the Name of a triune God, what does this teach us but that neither our children nor we can effect this purification that is so necessary and thus we have to seek this purification outside of ourselves? But where then should a sinner seek for this cleansing of sin? Or from whom should he seek it? These questions are answered in the second part of the form where it speaks of deliverance. The form points to the triune covenant God.

The Washing Away of Sins
Secondly. Holy baptism witnesseth and sealeth unto us the washing away of our sins through Jesus Christ.

In baptism, deliverance is visibly preached. There is deliverance! There is a sequel to the first part! This is a wonder in itself. The first part, dealing with our misery, was from ourselves and by ourselves. We robbed ourselves of all our gifts and have made ourselves utterly miserable, perverse, and corrupt.

The second part, dealing with deliverance, is from and by God. It is a fruit of His eternal thoughts of love. This is the wonder that the people of God cannot comprehend—namely, that there is deliverance for condemnable sinners. Concerning the fallen angels, the devils, nothing remained but to be "reserved in everlasting chains under darkness unto the judgment of the great day" (Jude 6). But for fallen man there is deliverance. The abyss of misery into which the authors have allowed us to look was terribly deep. We shuddered when we cast a glance into the abyss wherein we have cast ourselves and our children.

However, the height of deliverance, which is now described by the authors, is greater than the depth of misery. Grace triumphs over guilt. The form says that this deliverance is *witnessed* and *sealed* in holy baptism. Baptism witnesses and seals. These are words that appear again and again in the Reformed doctrine of the sacraments. What does witnessing mean? Witnessing is convincing someone of a certain truth. The Lord says in Psalm 50:7, "Hear, O my people, and I will speak, O Israel, and I will testify[1] against thee: I am God, even thy God." We find witnessing clearly set forth in Peter's sermon on the day of Pentecost: "And with many other words did he testify [witness] and exhort, saying, save yourselves from this untoward generation" (Acts 2:40). In baptism, we are confronted with God's witnessing. He testifies with great emphasis of the washing away of sin in the blood of Christ and of the firmness of His unmovable covenant.

In baptism, God not only witnesses, but also seals. The form speaks of witnessing and sealing. What is sealing? To seal something means to put a personal, authenticating mark upon it. This is common in trade. When a contract is made and a deed is written, a seal is affixed to the deed to confirm its authenticity. A

---

[1] Dutch: "witness."

seal is also affixed to something to confirm ownership. Seals were affixed to cattle and even to slaves. A seal on merchandise is evidence of authenticity. Sealing confirms genuineness and truth. In baptism, God seals the truth of His covenant and His promises. That is the nature and essence of baptism.

Holy baptism is a sacrament. The Heidelberg Catechism tells us what a sacrament is: "The sacraments are holy visible signs and seals, appointed of God for this end, that by the use thereof, he may the more fully declare and seal to us the promise of the gospel" (Q. 66).

The Lord instituted these signs and seals for our sake. The promises He has given in His Word are most reliable; therefore, they do not need sealing. But our faith is weak and small. Considering this, the Lord has given the sacraments in addition to the Word. Thus, the sacraments have not been instituted as if God's Word alone is not sufficient or trustworthy, for "God is not a man, that he should lie; neither the son of man, that he should repent" (Num. 23:19). True believers are often weak in faith. Faith is tried, and the regenerate often do not dare to accept God's promises and apply them to themselves. But see how the Lord takes into account that weak faith and says, "I assure you through these visible signs that there is eternal righteousness and salvation in My Son for poor, hell-worthy sinners, who with Ephraim smite upon their thigh because of their sin." The Lord has affixed the sacraments as seals to His Word. The sacraments do not offer a different message than the Word, but they confirm the message of the Word.

The Belgic Confession of Faith says in Article 33, "We believe that our gracious God, on account of our weakness and infirmities hath ordained the sacraments for us, thereby to seal unto us his promises, and to be pledges of the good will and grace of God toward us, and also to nourish and strengthen our faith; which he hath joined to the Word of the gospel." To understand this correctly with regard to holy baptism, we must go back to the sacrament of circumcision in the Old Testament. God made His covenant with Abraham. We read in Genesis

17:7 that the content of this covenant was, "And I will establish my covenant between me and thee and thy seed after thee in their generations for an everlasting covenant, to be a God unto thee, and to thy seed after thee." After this covenant was made, the Lord said to Abraham, "This is my covenant, which ye shall keep, between me and you and thy seed after thee; Every man child among you shall be circumcised.... And it shall be a token of the covenant betwixt me and you" (Gen. 17:10-11). The Lord wanted to confirm the covenant and gave Abraham a visible pledge. This pledge, or seal, was circumcision. It was a visible sign of an invisible promise. It was given to strengthen the faith of Abraham and to assure him of the truth of the covenant that God had made with him and his seed. Circumcision, therefore, pointed back to that covenant of God with Abraham. It was a sign and a seal of that covenant and of what was promised in it. We find the same thing in holy baptism. In Colossians 2:11, the apostle calls this "the circumcision of Christ."

Baptism fulfills the same purpose as circumcision; it is a pledge and seal of that which is promised. It is a pledge of the same covenant as circumcision was—namely, of the eternal covenant of grace in which God granted eternal salvation to His elect in Christ. Just as the Lord sealed the truth and faithfulness of His covenant to His church of the Old Testament in circumcision, He seals the same to His church of the New Testament in baptism. Baptism is a sacrament that testifies and seals. Luther says, "This is how it is done in worldly testaments—not only are the words written down, but also seals or signs are affixed, so that it will always be sure and reliable. In this Testament, Christ did likewise. He affixed to the Word a powerful and very precious seal and sign."

The terms *witnessing* and *sealing* touch the heart of the doctrine of the sacraments. Separated from the Word, they are meaningless. They do not proclaim new things. The sacraments confirm the truth and the faithfulness of God's promises. God does not lie; His promises are "yea and amen." Faith must find its assurance here and nowhere else.

What then does baptism witness and seal? The authors say, "The washing away of our sins in Jesus Christ." To call baptism a testimony of the washing away of sins is a biblical expression. In Acts 22, Ananias said to Paul, "And now why tarriest thou? arise, and be baptized, and wash away thy sins, calling on the name of the Lord." Baptism points to a washing. Paul speaks in Titus 3 of "the washing of regeneration, and renewing of the Holy Ghost." The sinner needs to be washed from sin, and baptism testifies of that washing away of sins. It pictures purification from the filth of sin and payment for sin through Christ's blood and Spirit. Blood—not the blood of bullocks or goats, but the blood of Jesus Christ, God's Son—is required for the washing away of sin. Only His blood can cleanse and forgive. What the law could not obtain, Christ did obtain through the shedding of His blood—namely, the washing away of sin.

In the first part, the water of baptism testified, "You require purification: you are unclean!" The water of baptism now testifies that purification is possible. It points to the blood of Christ that cleanses from all sin, and thus testifies that the greatest of sinners can be washed from sin in the blood of Christ. Baptism not only testifies of this, but also *seals* it. It visibly preaches the truth that "the blood of Jesus Christ his Son cleanseth us from all sin" (1 John 1:7).

As water washes away the impurity of the body, so the blood of Christ washes away the impurity of the soul. The power of Christ's blood is proclaimed whenever the gospel is preached. In baptism, this gospel is made visible; that is why baptism is sometimes called a *visible gospel*. Everything proclaims, "The blood of Jesus Christ his Son cleanseth us from all sin."

Notice that we do not read that baptism *is* the washing away of sin. Baptism itself does not effect the washing away of sin, but it symbolizes that washing away. It signifies and seals this. It does not promise any other purification than that accomplished by the sprinkling with the blood of Christ. Of this, baptism is a sign and a seal. The water of baptism depicts the washing away of sin through the blood of Jesus Christ. It testifies that no sinner can be too impure or too filthy for the blood of Christ to cleanse from sin.

The sacrament of baptism also has a sealing power. Sacraments are not only signs, but also seals. Scripture calls them seals of the righteousness of faith (Rom. 4:11). The promises of the covenant of grace are powerfully confirmed and sealed through the sacraments. If only this were realized more often! Then sacraments would regain their true function in the life of faith. God's children rob themselves, partly through ignorance, of much comfort and the strength of faith by failing to see the purpose of the sacraments as instituted by Christ. Sometimes God's people obtain very little comfort and strengthening from the administration of holy baptism. Through the sacrament of the Lord's Supper, faith is strengthened, but the fact that the Lord instituted the sacrament of holy baptism for the same purpose is often not perceived.

We ought to pay special attention to this deep meaning of the sacrament of holy baptism. Rev. G. H. Kersten correctly and strongly points this out when he says, "In baptism, God confirms His covenant unto the salvation of His elect and to the comfort of all His people" (*Compendium*, p. 116).

The authors say that the great promise and substance of the covenant of grace sealed in baptism is "the washing away of sins through the blood of Jesus Christ." This is the substance of God's salvation. This washing away of sins through the blood of Christ is sacramentally sealed in baptism, and thereby contains a source of comfort and strength for faith for God's church.

Let us look at this a bit further. The regenerated sinner has learned through the working of the Holy Spirit to understand what the authors put before us in the first part: "That we are conceived and born in sin, insomuch that we cannot enter into the kingdom of God." The sinner convicted by the Holy Spirit is bowed down under a burden of guilt and sin. In particular, indwelling sin is a cause of great sorrow and distress. He experiences with David, "For mine iniquities are gone over mine head: as an heavy burden they are too heavy for me. My wounds stink and are corrupt because of my foolishness" (Ps. 38:4-5). The law curses and God's righteousness demands his death. Sometimes Satan stands at his right hand, pointing to his filthy garments, just as he did to Joshua. Then this guilty sinner hears the preaching or reads in the Scriptures of the promises of the gospel. He hears that there is reconciliation and purification in the blood of Christ. This message is like water on a thirsty desert and glad tidings from a far country. Amid the distress of his heart, he hears, "The blood of Jesus Christ his Son cleanseth us from all sin." Because of the greatness of his guilt and the realization of the corruption of his heart, he can scarcely believe that these promises are for someone such as he, so he is tossed back and forth between hope and fear. Sinai's thundering can frighten so much and the conscience can accuse such a sinner so terribly that he cannot lay hold of the promises of the gospel. The sinner hears of the riches in Christ preached to him, and the great blessings of God's covenant and the power of the blood of Christ are offered to him, but the multitude of objections is too large for him to get through in order to touch the hem of Christ's garment, as the woman who had the issue of blood. With Abraham, he cries out when he hears the promises of the gospel, "Whereby shall I know it?"

These are the people whom the Lord wants to reassure through baptism. He descends from heaven, as it were, and fixes His seal on His covenant and on His promises, confirming in baptism their reliability and truth. He vows with a visible oath that what they have heard is true, to their astonishment—namely, that the blood of Christ His Son cleanses from all sin. He breaks through all their fear and says, "Do you see the water being sprinkled on the infant? So certainly the blood of Christ My Son cleanses from all sin." To such guilty ones it is proclaimed, "Be of good cheer, the Master is here and He calls you."

The Lord said to Abraham, "Look up at the stars"; to Gideon, "Look at the fleece of wool"; and to Hezekiah, "Look at the dial of Ahaz." To the fearful sinner who stands back, the Lord says, "Look at the water sprinkled upon the head of the infant. Hear thereby the swearing of an oath and the promises of a triune God, for so assuredly I do confirm that in Christ's blood there is washing and purification for a condemnable sinner as you."

Oh, how this makes guilty sinners go out to God! This makes them flee to that pure Fountain and cry out, "See, here is water; what doth hinder me to be baptized?" (Acts 8:36). Baptism preaches to those who are afraid of God's holy justice and who are afraid to believe that, despite Christ's satisfaction, God will not be angry anymore. This provides unspeakable strength for the faith of God's children. The sure foundation and truth of God's covenant and of His promises are visibly presented to them and sustain their faith.

The testament is opened through the death of the Son of God, and, with wonder, guilty sinners read their names in it. Thus, through the sacrament, God's children receive a sacramental assurance of their interest in Christ. They are given a favorable assurance by God of their interest in God's eternal covenant of grace.

What the Heidelberg Catechism says in Question 69 becomes true: "How art thou admonished and assured by holy baptism, that the one sacrifice of Christ upon the cross is of real advantage to thee? Thus: That Christ appointed this external washing with water, adding thereto this promise, that I am as certainly washed by his blood and Spirit from all the pollution of my soul, that is, from all my sins, as I am washed externally with water, by which the filthiness of the body is commonly washed away." The sacrament of baptism then serves its true function: to strengthen faith by sealing the promises of God.

This sure ground outside of ourselves is not only pointed out to us, but the faithfulness and truth thereof are also sealed and confirmed. God fixes His seal to the promises He has made. This is the great substance of the words of the authors that holy baptism "seals the washing away of sins through Jesus Christ."

Everyone will understand that the benefit of that sacramental sealing is obtained through faith alone. We must use this seal through faith; only then does the sacrament have its sealing power. Baptism is a seal of God's covenant of grace, but this seal becomes fruitful only when the Holy Spirit grants the sinner to accept it by faith. Calvin says, "The sacraments duly perform their office only when accompanied by the Spirit, the internal Master, whose energy alone penetrates the heart, stirs up the affections, and procures access for the sacraments into our souls" (*Institutes*, 4.14.9).

Only the Holy Spirit can work the sealing of God's grace in us. According to Calvin, there is an outward sealing in the sacraments, but the inward confirmation of that sealing is through the Holy Spirit. Calvin also teaches that the Holy Spirit works through the use of the means of grace. The Holy Spirit uses the sacrament to assure the sinner in his doubts and fears that God is gracious—gracious even for me. He shows us that the blood of Jesus cleanses from all sin, even all my sin. Through the promises of God in particular, confirmed through the sacraments, assurance is worked in the heart. In our deepest distress, no other ground of assurance remains other than the promises of God. Amid the strife (whether or not it seems that God's promise is true, and especially whether or not it is true for *me*), the Holy Spirit assures us through the sacraments of the truth and trust-worthiness of the promises of the gospel. Whoever may rest in this, rests upon the same ground as that on which Abraham rested in all his struggles—upon God, who cannot lie.

The sacrament encourages us to entrust ourselves in this manner to God and His promises. The holy art of holding fast to God's promises in all distress and strife is what Scripture calls *faith*. Such faith goes against all that it feels, sees, and observes. It holds fast to the promising and promise-sealing God, who cannot lie. This brings the heart to fully surrender to the oath-taking God and say, "Behold, we come unto thee; for thou art the LORD our God" (Jer. 3:22).

Faith is required for the sacrament. The Word serves to work faith and the sacrament serves to strengthen faith. Therefore, faith must be present. Without faith, we do not profit from the sacrament. Calvin says, "They confer nothing, and avail nothing, if not received in faith, just as wine and oil, or any other liquid, however large the quantity you pour out, will run away and perish unless there be an open vessel to receive it. When the vessel is not open, though it may be sprinkled all over, it will nevertheless remain entirely empty" (*Institutes*, 4.14.17). Speaking of sealing in baptism, Ursinus says, "By mixing the water with faith upon the sealed promises, the benefit thereof is obtained." Through God's sealing in baptism, faith is strengthened so much that we can agree with Paul: "Neither death, nor life, nor angels, nor principalities, nor powers, nor things present, nor things to come, nor height, nor depth, nor any other creature, shall be able to separate us from the love of God, which is in Christ Jesus our Lord" (Rom. 8:38-39).

To close this declaration of baptism—that the blood of Christ cleanses of all sin—I would like to ask, "Is it possible for God to say more clearly than He has said in baptism that there is forgiveness and purification for you?" Never forget this and do not allow the devil to rob you of your assurance of it. You are baptized; it is sealed on your forehead that the blood of Christ cleanses from all sin.

A God of Full Salvation

Therefore we are baptized in the name of the Father, and of the Son, and of the Holy Ghost.

There is a reason why baptism is administered in the name of the Father, the Son, and the Holy Spirit. The authors of the form for the administration of baptism say, "Therefore..." and refer to the preceding part, which said that holy baptism witnesses and seals unto us the washing away of our sins through Jesus Christ. We are therefore baptized in the name of the Father and of the Son and of the Holy Spirit to witness and seal the washing away of sins in the blood of Jesus Christ. Baptism concerns the sealing of the promise; this is the meaning of the sacraments. The promise is the central part. The sacrament is only added to the promise to seal and confirm it. Baptism introduces nothing new, but only seals what God has already promised in the gospel and in the covenant of grace.

Calvin says, "We conclude, therefore, that the sacraments are truly termed evidences of divine grace, and, as it were, seals of the goodwill which he entertains toward us. They, by sealing it to us, sustain, nourish, confirm, and increase our faith" (*Institutes*, 4.14.7). This is one of God's mercies. God's truth is sure and steadfast in itself. The sacrament is not added to the Word of God as if God's promises were uncertain. It is our faith that needs to be supported, not the Word of God. Our faith is small and weak; the sacraments serve to encourage this weak faith. Therefore, baptism is administered in the name of the Father and of the Son and of the Holy Spirit. In the unabridged form for the administration of baptism used prior to 1574, we read, "And to the end that He would confirm such a promise to our weak faith and seal it to our own bodies, He has commanded that we be baptized in the name of God, of the Father and of the Son and of the Holy Ghost."

To confirm the promises of the gospel to our weak faith, baptism is administered in the name of the Father and of the Son and of the Holy Spirit. If baptism were administered in the name of the church or of any person, faith would not dare to rest upon God's promise. God connects His name to baptism in order to support the faith in the promise, and His promise is sealed in the name of the triune God. The baptismal formula of Matthew 28:19 reads, "In the name of the Father, and of the Son, and of the Holy Ghost."

"In the name of" implies a revelation of God. In Scripture, the name of the Lord signifies the Lord Himself. Baptism seals the promises in the name of God, and, particularly in the New Testament, this is the triune God.

Writing on the expression, "In the name of the Father, and of the Son, and of the Holy Ghost" (Matt. 28:19), Calvin says, "That a full and clear knowledge of God, which had been but darkly shadowed out under the Law and the Prophets, is at length fully discovered under the reign of Christ." Calvin then continues, "There are good reasons why the Father, the Son, and the Holy Spirit, are expressly mentioned; for there is no other way in which the efficacy of baptism can be experienced than when we begin with the unmerited mercy of the Father, who reconciles us with himself by the only begotten Son; next Christ comes forward with the sacrifice of his death; and at length, the Holy Spirit is likewise added, by whom he washes and regenerates us (Titus 3:5), and, in short, makes us partakers of his benefits." In both the covenant of grace and in baptism, a seal of the covenant of grace, we are dealing with a triune God.

What then does the triune God witness and confirm in baptism? The authors of the form provide us with the answer when they profess:

> For when we are baptized in the name of the Father, God the Father witnesseth and sealeth unto us that he doth make an eternal covenant of grace with us, and adopts us for his children and heirs, and therefore will provide us with every good thing, and avert all evil or turn it to our profit. And when we are baptized in the name of the Son, the Son sealeth unto us that he doth wash us in his blood from all our sins, incorporating us into the fellowship of his death and resurrection, so that we are freed from all our sins, and accounted righteous before God. In like manner, when we are baptized in the name of the Holy Ghost, the Holy Ghost assures us, by this holy sacrament, that he will dwell in us, and sanctify us to be members of Christ, applying unto us that which we have in Christ, namely, the washing away of our sins, and the daily renewing of our lives, till we shall finally shall be presented without spot or wrinkle among the assembly of the elect in life eternal.

We are listening to a promising God: God the Father, God the Son, and God the Holy Spirit. Each Person of the Godhead is speaking in holy baptism. The deliverance of sinners is anchored in the covenant dealings of the three Persons in the Godhead. Each Person fulfills His own part in the execution of the covenant; it is a joint work of all three. In baptism, each of the three Persons of the Godhead commits Himself to the covenant so that the elect can fully possess their benefits.

God the Father witnesses and seals, God the Son seals, and God the Holy Spirit confirms. Each of the divine Persons will work what is necessary unto the salvation of the elect and will fulfill the promise, "I will be a God unto thee."

When We Are Baptized

The part that we will now discuss begins each time with the phrase: "when we are baptized." What takes place when we are baptized in the name of the Father, and of the Son, and of the Holy Ghost?

From what we read in the form, it appears that God the Father, God the Son, and God the Holy Ghost witness and seal. The question is *what* and *to whom* do they witness and seal? We will try to give an answer by carefully considering what the form says.

Who is meant by *we* and *us?* Let us listen to the pre-1574 unabridged form: "Therefore, in the first place, when He wants us to be baptized with water in the name of the Father, He witnesseth unto us, as with a visible oath, that during our whole life, He wants to be a Father to us and our children...." The form emphasizes "to us and our children." When it mentions what God the Son promises, we read again, "to us and our children." And when it speaks of the Holy Spirit, it says again, "to us and our children." This shows us that baptism concerns both us and our children. Baptism is neither a private matter between the parents and the minister, nor a matter that concerns only the child. It concerns "us and our children"—the congregation and her seed. All that the Father, the Son, and the Holy Spirit witness and seal in baptism is witnessed and sealed to the congregation with her children.

Thus baptism is a sign and seal of God's covenant. God the Father, God the Son, and God the Holy Ghost undertake to fulfill what is promised in the covenant. Through baptism, God's promises are sealed to the Christian church, just as circumcision sealed God's covenant and promises unto Israel.

You may ask, "Is the Christian church allowed to lay a claim to that which the Lord had promised unto Abraham and his seed? Has baptism truly replaced circumcision and the congregation of the New Testament replaced Israel?"

In Colossians 2:11-12 and Romans 4 and 6, the association between baptism and circumcision is emphasized. Baptism is seen as the fulfillment of circumcision. The seal has been changed, but the covenant remains the same. Calvin particularly emphasized this. To Calvin, there is only one covenant; the covenant of grace is indeed revealed in different forms, but in essence it is one and the same covenant. For this reason, he could emphasize that the Christian church has come in the place of the Old Testament Israel. It therefore follows that what was confirmed and sealed to Israel in circumcision is now sealed to the Christian church in baptism. In his *Institutes*, Calvin says,

> Scripture gives us a still clearer knowledge of the truth. For it is most evident that the covenant, which the Lord once made with Abraham, is not less applicable to Christians now than it was anciently to the Jewish people, and therefore that word (God's promise to Abraham, "And I will establish my covenant between me and thee and thy seed after thee in their generations for an everlasting covenant, to be a God unto thee, and to thy seed after thee") has no less reference to Christians than to Jews. Unless, indeed, we imagine that Christ, by his advent, diminished, or curtailed the grace of the Father—an idea not free from execrable blasphemy. Wherefore, both the children of the Jews, because, when made heirs of that covenant, they were separated from the heathen, were called a holy seed, and for the same reason the children of Christians, or those who have only one believing parent, are called holy, and, by the testimony of the apostle (1 Corinthians 7:14), differ from the impure seed of idolaters.

According to Calvin, whose influence permeates this form, the same promises that applied to circumcision now apply to baptism.

An objection may be raised that the Lord made a covenant with only the elect from Abraham's seed and that the promise of baptism will be fulfilled at God's time in the elect only. Indeed, the essence of the covenant concerns God's elect only. God's promises are fulfilled in them and to them. But that is only known to God.

Therefore, Calvin clearly opposes those who say that the covenant has been made only with the elect from Abraham's seed. According to Scripture, the covenant has been established with Abraham and his natural seed. Calvin is too scriptural to let this pass unnoticed, even though he says that the promises are fulfilled in the elect only and that, according to Galatians 3:29, only true believers are the true seed of Abraham.

In his commentary on Genesis 17:7, Calvin says,

> There is no doubt that the Lord distinguishes the race of Abraham from the rest of the world. We must now see what people he intends. Now they are deceived who think that his elect alone are here pointed out; and that all the faithful are indiscriminately comprehended, from whatever people, according to the flesh, they are descended. For, on the contrary, the Scripture declares that the race of Abraham, by lineal descent, had been peculiarly accepted by God.

Further, Calvin's argument holds no contradiction between God's election and His establishing of a covenant with all descendants of Abraham and the entire visible church. He makes this clear by referring to two distinct types of children in Israel and in the visible church. First, there are children of the covenant who bear the sign of the covenant and to whom God solemnly and willingly offers His grace, but who are only children of the flesh. They remain strangers to the grace of regeneration and of faith in Christ. But second, the true children of Abraham are they who through regeneration and faith have become partakers of Christ and of all His benefits. Calvin says that this distinction flows forth from the fountain of sovereign election.

Biblically, we must bring in election here. The true partakers of the covenant do not distinguish themselves, but are distinguished by God's gracious election. This election flows through the channel and administration of the covenant, which in the Old Testament encompassed Israel and in the New Testament encompasses the visible church.

God's covenant of grace is the channel through which the stream of election flows. The Lord fulfils His counsel in the bosom of the church. Even though the elect are the real partakers of the covenant, the administration of the covenant applies to all Israel and the entire Christian church. God's sovereign election makes the distinction. We may not and cannot make that distinction. We only know that the Lord has promised to keep His covenant with Abraham and his seed for a thousand generations.

Likewise, we know that the Lord promised His church, "I will be thy God and the God of thy seed." According to God's sovereignty, this does not mean that every baptized person will be saved. That is not the meaning behind the confirmation and sealing in baptism. Rather, baptism seals the truth of God's promise that He will keep His covenant and will gather from the children of the visible church a church unto eternal life. God's promise to His church is sealed in baptism, and He will keep covenant with His church. The continuation of the church lies firm in the faithful promises of God.

Because God confirms His covenant throughout all generations, the church will continue to exist, and therefore, we baptize. This expectation leans on God's promise to believers that He will be their God and the God of their seed. God's promises to keep His covenant are not dependent on human conditions; the God of the covenant of grace promises to work in His elect what is necessary to become true partakers of the covenant.

The church is more than a society. It is God's covenant people, even as Israel was. Baptism offers comfort to the congregation. God has made His covenant with her and He will confirm this covenant throughout all generations.

Baptism concerns "us and our children." We read in Lord's Day 27 of the Heidelberg Catechism, Question 74, "Are infants also to be baptized?" The answer is, "Yes: for since they, as well as the adult, are included in the covenant and church of God; and since redemption from sin by the blood of Christ, and the Holy Ghost, the author of faith, is promised to them no less than to the adult...."

The Belgic Confession of Faith is in agreement with this. It also emphasizes God's promise sealed in baptism unto the church and her children. Regarding infant baptism, Article 34 states that the Anabaptists condemn the baptism of the infants of believers, but we believe "they ought to be baptized and sealed with the sign of the covenant, as the children in Israel formerly were circumcised, upon the same promises which are made unto our children." Thus, the Belgic Confession of Faith also says that the same promises that God confirmed to Israel in circumcision are now confirmed to the children of the Christian church through baptism. Following the example of Calvin, the covenant line connects Israel to the New Testament church.

Baptism has come in the place of circumcision and the Christian church has come in the place of Israel. The promises which were confirmed to Israel through circumcision are now confirmed to the New Testament church and to her seed through baptism. God's church now consists of Jews and Gentiles.

Whenever baptism is administered, God's promise—"I will be thy God and the God of thy seed"—is sealed. God Himself then undertakes to keep what He promised in the covenant.

Calvin's catechism (1537) says, "The right to baptize our children is founded on this, that they also are party to the eternal covenant, in which the Lord promises that he will be a God, not only unto us, but also unto our seed." Again, this does not mean that each child automatically is or will be born again, but rather that God will fulfill His promises to the church and to her seed. According to His sovereign will, God passes by Ishmael and adopts Isaac; He loves Jacob and hates Esau. Although God's reasons are hidden from us, yet we do know that God promises and seals in baptism that He will fulfill His covenant and His promises to the church. You may not say, "This is only of value to the elect children of the church." Then you begin to deal with things that are hidden from us. Luther compared the hidden predestination and the revealed Word of God to a ladder connecting heaven and earth. The top rung is predestination and reaches into the heights of heaven; the lowest rung is God's gospel promise that stands next to us on the earth. When we want to begin with the uppermost rung, Luther said, we will break our neck; we must begin with the lowest rung—i.e., with God's gracious promise.

Baptism relates to the reprobate also. Calvin discusses this problem in his commentary on Titus 3:5 and says, "Although by baptism wicked men are neither washed nor renewed, yet it retains that power, so far as relates to God, because, although they reject the grace of God, still it is offered to them." If you ask, "But how can the sacrament be a confirmation of God's promise for a reprobate?" then Calvin answers, "It is irrational to contend that the sacraments are not manifestations of divine grace toward us, because they are held forth to the ungodly also, who, however, so far from experiencing God to be more propitious to them, only incur greater condemnation. By the same reasoning, the gospel will be no manifestation of the grace of God, because it is spurned by many who hear it" (*Institutes*, 4.14.7).

In accord with God's sovereignty, not all those called Israel are Israel; many are not partakers of the essence of the covenant. Yet, God has promised to His congregation, "I will be a God unto thee and to thy seed after thee in their generations." This unspeakable comfort provides hope for the generations to come.

The men at the national synod at Dordrecht confided much in God, who testifies and seals in baptism that He is faithful regarding His covenant and promises through the children of the church. They comforted godly parents who mourned over the loss of young children with these covenant promises of God; the Canons, Head I, Article 17 says, "Since we are to judge of the will of God from his Word, which testifies that the children of believers are holy, not by nature, but in virtue of the covenant of grace, in which they, together with the parents, are comprehended, godly parents have no reason to doubt of the election and salvation of their children, whom it pleaseth God to call out of this life in their infancy" (Gen. 17:7, Acts 2:39, 1 Cor. 7:14). Therefore, baptism is a pleading ground for the conversion of our children.

We have thus seen how God testifies and seals His covenant and promises to the church through baptism. In His sovereignty it will not be applied unto every child of the church, but His electing and saving dealings will be manifested in the church.

I conclude this section by quoting Rev. G. H. Kersten: "Thus baptism remains a sign and seal that the Lord remembers His covenant forever; that He will be our God and the God of our seed to a thousand generations, according to His good pleasure, not always glorifying His grace from parent to child, but gathering His elect out of the natural generations to one spiritual generation, in which the great covenant grace of salvation is confirmed, 'I shall be their God and they shall be my people.'" (*Reformed Dogmatics*, 2:517).

Concerning God the Father

For when we are baptized in the name of the Father, God the Father witnesseth and sealeth unto us, that he doth make an eternal covenant of grace with us.

In baptism, God the Father promises to make an eternal covenant of grace. We read there with emphasis: "He doth make!" He makes an eternal covenant of grace.

We speak of a one-sided covenant. It becomes two-sided—that is, involving covenant responsibilities on the parts of both God and the believer—only after it is established. The establishment of the covenant of grace with a fallen sinner is one-sided.

After the fall, Adam fled tremblingly from God. The

covenant of works, and consequently the good and blessed relationship with God, was broken. When a new covenant was
revealed (Gen. 3:15) to replace the covenant of works, the ini-
tiative did not come from man. Adam had fled after the
covenant of works had been broken; only God could initiate a
new covenant.

We observe the same thing with Abraham. The Lord called
Abraham, and said, "I will establish my covenant between me
and thee and thy seed after thee in their generations for an everlasting covenant, to be a God unto thee, and to thy seed after
thee." Did Abraham ask for this? No, he did not. Joshua 24:2
reveals that Abraham had served other gods before the Lord
made a covenant with him.

Grace is one-sided, as befits the character of the covenant of
grace. In this covenant, God cares for everything. Therefore,
God makes this covenant "an eternal covenant of grace." God
did not first make a covenant of works with Adam and then
later create a new one with Abraham and his posterity. A
covenant of grace was made. Grace is the origin, the content,
and the goal of this covenant; everything in it breathes of grace.

The covenant of grace is the revelation of God's eternal
love. Through this covenant, God brings the sinner into a new
and reconciled relationship with Himself. Behind the covenant
of grace is the decree of God's eternal and undeserved election.
God's election not only concerns its recipients, but it also concerns the means whereby fallen sinners are to be restored into
His communion. This would be accomplished through Christ's
satisfaction of His Father's justice. Christ is at the center of
election as the chosen Savior. This makes clear that the
covenant of grace and election involve the same mission: the
ingathering and salvation of sinners, elected by God, through
the Mediator, Christ. Thus, the covenant of grace and election
are closely connected. The covenant of grace brings the realization and work of election in time. The words "makes an eternal
covenant of grace" indicate that the decree made in eternity
comes to pass in time. God's eternal election becomes reality

through the covenant of grace. Election is made visible on earth in the covenant.

The covenant of grace, revealed in time and extending from generation to generation, performs the eternal counsel of God, or the covenant of redemption. Election is the heart and kernel of the covenant of grace. Thus, there is no contradiction between election and the covenant of grace. Rev. Kersten may say in his *Reformed Dogmatics*, "The covenant of grace is the execution of the covenant of redemption that was made with the elect in Christ their representative Head. In essence they are both the same. If we make a difference it is only in this respect that the covenant of redemption is the eternal immanent working from eternity, and the covenant of grace is the performance of it eminently, immediately after the fall" (ch. 20).

Thus, the covenant of grace is not a different covenant from that made between Christ, as the Head of the elect, and the Father, representing the three divine Persons; it is only the performance of that covenant in time. The covenant of grace incorporates sinners into that covenant in time. This incorporation started with Adam and will finish with the last elect person on this earth.

Now, what does God say in baptism? The form for the administration of baptism says, "God the Father witnesseth and sealeth unto us, that he doth make an eternal covenant of grace with us, and adopts us for his children and heirs."

We have seen that this concerns Abraham and his posterity. We read in Genesis 17 that an *eternal* covenant of grace was established—that is, an unbreakable covenant. This means that it will never be annulled; it holds eternal truths and it exists from eternity. Election is its foundation. There is rich comfort in the permanence of God's covenant. We sing about this when baptism is administered: "Jehovah's truth will stand forever, His covenant-bonds He will not sever."

The adoption of the children of God is promised in this eternal covenant. The authors say, "adopts us for his children and heirs." The bond of the covenant of grace that the Lord makes with sinners from the fallen race of Adam is very strong. It is not the bond of a mighty ruler who makes a covenant with a poor shabby beggar, but of a holy and righteous God who, as a loving Father, adopts slaves of hell for His beloved children. "And [I] will be a Father unto you, and ye shall be my sons and daughters, saith the Lord Almighty" (2 Cor. 6:18). This is the great promise of the covenant of grace: through Christ, God has reconciled His church with Himself and adopted them for His children.

This is why Abraham was called the friend of God (James 2:23). The wonder described by Hosea becomes real when God, through regenerating grace, makes a covenant of grace with a sinner. The words of Hosea 1:10 are fulfilled: "And it shall come to pass, that in the place where it was said unto them, Ye are not my people, there it shall be said unto them, Ye are the sons of the living God." Here the new covenant exceeds the old covenant.

Abraham was called a friend of God. For Jesus' sake, God now calls His church beloved children and heirs. Through Adam's fall, they became the slaves of hell and children of wrath, but, through the grace of His covenant, they are adopted as children of God.

"Adopted," says the form. Because of Christ's satisfaction, they are incorporated into the family of God. It is adoption because of grace and because it is for Christ's sake. The price paid to give this adoption to fallen and hell-worthy sinners was high—the death of the only begotten Son of God. Jesus, as the proper Child of the Father, could no longer say "Father" in the hour of His death, but cried out, "My God, my God, why hast thou forsaken me?"

How great is the unfathomable love of God that is the foundation of this confession: "adopts us for his children and heirs." Baptism is a seal and a pledge of this gracious adoption. In it, God testifies and seals that He adopts us for His children and heirs. God says in baptism, "I will be a Father unto you, and you shall be My sons and daughters."

But the question is, "Will this grace be applied to all who are baptized, without distinction?" The history of the people of

Israel teaches us that this is not the case, and we see it confirmed in the New Testament as well. Esau despised God's covenant. The branches that do not bear fruit will be burned. Many who are baptized prove to be children of the flesh only and are not of the faith of Abraham.

How is this possible when God's promises are never void? Many solve this problem by saying that God's promises are conditional—the fulfillment of the promises depends on certain conditions to be fulfilled by man. Many say that the covenant of grace does nothing more than offer the promises to all who are baptized, thereby translating the covenant of grace into merely an offer of salvation.

Now it is true that there is an offer of salvation in baptism because the truth of God's promises of grace are sealed by it. The sacrament is affixed as a seal to the gospel. Calvin says, "He, therefore, who would thoroughly understand the effect of baptism—its object and true character—must not stop short at the element and corporeal object, but look forward to the divine promises which are therein offered to us" (*Institutes*, 4.16.2).

Yet, at the same time, the covenant of grace is much more than a revelation and an offer of the salvation found in Christ. The covenant of grace is the promise that the Lord "will be a God unto you." He gives Himself to His elect to be their God and He adopts them for His people. The covenant grants and promises all that is necessary for salvation.

When conditions have to be fulfilled, a promise is no longer certain. But God's covenant promise does not depend on us fulfilling conditions. We cannot fulfill anything. Our capability does not extend beyond rejecting the promise. If the promise were dependent on conditions to be fulfilled by man, such as repentance and faith, it would never be fulfilled. The promises are fulfilled through repentance and faith, but they are not the conditions on which the fulfillment is dependent. Conditions interfere with the character of the covenant of grace. In the covenant of grace God says, "*I* shall make My covenant." It is

God who makes it—sovereignly, one-sidedly, and graciously. He takes care of the realization of the promise.

The covenant of grace is not just a promise of a new relationship between God and a sinner, possible only if man fulfills certain conditions, such as believing and accepting the given promise. No, the covenant of grace is "I shall make." God will do it.

This promise's fulfillment is not dependent on Abraham believing the promise; that would make God dependent on man. The covenant with Abraham was established from one side, and it is no different in the New Testament. In the announcement of the new covenant God made, we read, "For this is the covenant that I will make with the house of Israel after those days, saith the Lord; I will put my laws into their mind, and write them in their hearts: and I will be to them a God, and they shall be to me a people" (Heb. 8:10). What is promised here is fundamental to the nature of the covenant. God does not make a promise dependent on our embrace of faith. It is quite the contrary. God promises to work everything necessary to be a true partaker of the covenant. Faith and repentance are promised; they are not demanded as conditions to be fulfilled by man. God promises to give what His covenant demands: faith and repentance.

In the covenant, God gives! God gives all that He can give, and that is Himself. This is the essence of the covenant: "I will be a God unto thee." However, there is a difficulty. God promises in baptism to make a covenant with believers and their seed, yet we know that this promise is not fulfilled in every baptized person. How can this be?

We could ask the same question with regard to the preaching of the Word. God comes earnestly with His offer of grace to all who hear the Word, and yet we see that one person repents and believes on Jesus while another does not.

Our answer must be that God's hidden and sovereign election makes this distinction. Election can never remove man's responsibility; but this way the honor of our conversion and faith is given to God's electing grace rather than to man.

The apostle Paul speaks in the same manner when he deals with God's covenant and promises, and the fulfillment of these promises in a remnant of Israel. In Romans 9, Paul answers how it is possible that the Israelites, who had the covenants and the promises, largely remained estranged from Christ. Many theologians answer, "Because they did not believe the promises of God and have rejected the offered gospel." And this is true. According to Scripture we must agree and we must preach this also. However, there is more to it! Israel's unbelief is only one side of the coin. Romans 9 teaches us that there is more involved. Israel had God's covenant and God's covenant promise: "I will be a God unto thee, and to thy seed after thee in their generations." They carried God's covenant in their flesh. Why then were these promises not fulfilled in a larger part of the people of Israel? The apostle goes back to God's election. Not all Israel was called Israel. God's covenant and promises do not deceive, but the elect "attained to righteousness" (v. 30). Any other solution is beyond our capability. We must profess both God's sovereign will and our responsibility. This also applies to God's covenant and promises.

Our responsibility weighs particularly heavy here. He who does not concern himself with God's covenant and its promises, and does not listen to the demand of that covenant, shall fall with Israel in the wilderness and not enter into Canaan because of his unbelief. However, sovereignty and undeserved grace are found in God's covenant which says, "I will...be gracious to whom I will be gracious, and will shew mercy on whom I will shew mercy" (Ex. 33:19).

Having discussed in detail the establishing of the covenant of grace, we conclude that God's election becomes visible in Abraham's descendants. God's promise is not empty.

Ultimately, salvation depends on God's election. God works in the elect by the hidden power of His Spirit so that they receive what the sacraments offer. We must not think that grace automatically accompanies the sacrament; the sovereignty of God's grace must be upheld. However, God will fulfill the promise made to the believers and their seed. As with Israel, God's election will become visible in the seed of the church. But within the church, not all will be Israel who are called Israel.

Meanwhile, we may not disregard God's promise. In particular, we must consider that God's promise speaks about generations; Scripture teaches that God works through generations. The promise, "I am thy God and the God of thy seed in their generations" is true; these are not empty words. We read in Psalm 106:45, "And he remembered for them his covenant, and repented according to the multitude of his mercies."

The separation between people by election, both within the covenant community of Israel and within the visible church, is directly related to God's sovereign good pleasure, which the elect receive. God's dealings, which we cannot comprehend, rest solely upon sovereign good pleasure. The Lord Jesus rejoiced in this sovereign good pleasure and said, "Even so, Father; for so it seemed good in thy sight" (Matt. 11:26). This good pleasure rests neither on our works nor on our believing; it rests on sovereign grace. This never means that unbelief and disobedience are excusable. The hidden election does not annul our responsibility or the command to repent and believe. The covenant of grace is not a testamentary fulfillment of an eternal decree whereby man is treated as a stone or a piece of wood. Its intention is that the sinner will repent and live. Baptism remains baptism, even though many reject it; similarly, the gospel remains the gospel even though it is rejected by many. It remains a faithful word, worthy of all acceptation. Thus, baptism is and remains a sign of God's goodwill toward us. The promise remains true even though it is only fulfilled in the elect. God is genuine when He says, "Seek Me and live!"

Let us end this part with a statement of Calvin: "Such is the value of the promise given to the posterity of Abraham; such the balance in which it is to be weighed. Hence, though we have no doubt that in distinguishing the children of God from bastards and foreigners, that the election of God reigns freely, we, at the same time, perceive that he was pleased specially to embrace the seed of Abraham with his mercy, and, for the better attestation of it, to seal it by circumcision. The case of the Christian church is entirely of the same description" (*Institutes*, 4.16.15).

As the form states as a matter of course, the following flows from this adoption by grace: "and therefore will provide us with every good thing, and avert all evil or turn it to our profit."

When God adopts sinners for His children, it follows that He will care for them as a good Father. He will show them fatherly love, provide them with every good thing, and avert all evil or turn it to their profit. Considering this, we would say, "But this is not the most important thing given to God's church in the covenant of grace, is it?" Indeed, the promise of God's favor and eternal communion is the most important aspect of the covenant of grace. But, in the covenant, God also regards as essential the temporal care for His people. The Lord does not consider our bodies as a side issue. The apostle even says, "That was not first which is spiritual, but that which is natural; and afterward that which is spiritual" (1 Cor. 15:46). Furthermore, the Lord Jesus taught that we are to pray first for daily bread and then for forgiveness of sins. The temporal life of God's children requires fatherly care. The Lord Jesus said, "For your heavenly Father knoweth that ye have need of all these things" (Matt. 6:32).

In Paradise, Adam was king over all created things, but through his transgression he lost all claims to the things of this earth. He not only lost life, but he also lost his claim to the fruits of the earth. The curse remains ours: "Thorns also and thistles shall it bring forth to thee" (Gen. 3:18). However, Christ merited for His church a renewed, sanctified claim to the things of this earth. God's children may now hear that the earth and its fullness are all theirs, because "ye are Christ's; and Christ is God's" (1 Cor. 3:23). God the Father measures out as much of this bountiful store of the earth as is necessary for them, merited for them by Christ. Their food and drink is anchored in God's covenant; the Lord will not withhold any good to them that walk uprightly.

Abraham was promised not only an eternal salvation, but also the possession of the land of Canaan for his descendants. The fear of the Lord brings forth fruit for this life as well as the life hereafter. Godliness has, according to Paul, the promise of the life that now is, and of that which is to come (1 Tim. 4:8).

The Lord will provide His children with "every good thing"—that is, with everything that is good for them. Sometimes we ask for things that are not at all good for us, and therefore we do not receive them. However, according to His faithful care, the Father gives us everything that is good. This should make us flee boldly to the faithful God and Father for our temporal needs. Believers may remind themselves of the word of the Lord Jesus, "Or what man is there of you, whom if his son ask bread, will he give him a stone? Or if he ask a fish, will he give him a serpent? If ye then, being evil, know how to give good gifts unto your children, how much more shall your Father which is in heaven give good things to them that ask him?" (Matt. 7:9-11).

God the Father also testifies and seals unto His church in baptism that He will "avert all evil or turn it to their profit." The Lord will not leave His church in times of cross bearing or in times of suffering, for He will turn all evil to their profit. They will enjoy His protection in this life of afflictions and miseries. The psalmist says, "For he shall give his angels charge over thee, to keep thee in all thy ways" (Ps. 91:11). The same God who wants to be their Sun to cherish and warm them also wants to be their Shield to protect them. And this kind care of God the Father over His church extends even to widows and orphans. The psalmist never saw the righteous forsaken, nor his seed begging bread (Ps. 37:25). They will lack nothing in this life. Suffering and oppression also come from His fatherly hand. Oh, how blessed is that people whose God is the Lord!

> *In evil times no shame they know,*
> *And in the days of famine's woe*
> *They shall be satisfied.*

The Lord desires to seal this and testify of it in baptism. For the true partakers of the covenant, the words of Romans 8:28 apply in all circumstances: "And we know that all things work together for good to them that love God, to them who are the called according to his purpose." Everything in this life will serve to the honor of their covenant God and the salvation of their souls, and all will end "through Him, through Him alone, because of His eternal good pleasure."

Concerning God the Son

Now that we have heard what God the Father confirms and seals in holy baptism, we have come to the part concerning God the Son. The form says, "When we are baptized in the name of the Son, the Son sealeth unto us, that he doth wash us in his blood from all our sins, incorporating us into the fellowship of his death and resurrection, so that we are freed from all our sins, and accounted righteous before God."

The work of reconciliation is the special role of the Son in the covenant of grace. Thus, in holy baptism, the propitiatory work of Christ is portrayed and sealed. The form emphatically points to the relationship between baptism and the sacrifice of Christ. In the eternal covenant of grace, the Son promised to become the Surety for His people — the Surety for all their guilt and transgressions. He saw that sacrifices and offerings could not satisfy, and said, "Lo, I come: in the volume of the book it is written of me, I delight to do thy will, O my God: yea, thy law is within my heart" (Ps. 40:7-8).

This is the agreement between the Father and the Son. Here Christ is the second Adam and the Surety of a better covenant. All the sins of the elect, both original and actual, before or after conversion, were charged to His account. He bowed Himself under their debt and under the curse of the law they had transgressed. He became their Surety and put Himself completely in their place. In the fullness of time, God laid all the iniquities of His people upon Him and required that He would give that which He took not away.

All the heavy demands of the law came on Christ so that all

the blessings of the covenant would come upon His church. He became her Redeemer and took her, with all her guilt and sin, onto His account. He put all her debt on His account and all His benefits were put to the account of His people. "For the transgression of my people was he stricken" (Isa. 58:1). Under the weight of the sin of His people, Jesus suffered the death of the cross and was laid in the grave. However, after having made atonement for the sins of His church through His propitiatory death, He rose from death and received from His Father a receipt of remission for all her sins. He who was delivered up for the sins of His church was raised up for her justification. In baptism this all is vividly demonstrated for us. Immersion in the water and rising out of it afterwards vividly portray Jesus' death and resurrection.

What does the Son declare in baptism regarding His reconciling death and justifying resurrection? Does He wish to merely portray His death and resurrection, or more than that?

The answer to that question lies in the form for the administration of baptism: "And when we are baptized in the name of the Son, the Son sealeth unto us, that he doth wash us in his blood from all our sins, incorporating us into the fellowship of his death and resurrection, so that we are freed from all our sins, and accounted righteous before God."

The form says that, in baptism, the Son seals. To what does Christ affix His seal in baptism? And what is it that He seals? In baptism, the Son seals the washing away of sin in His blood and our incorporation into His death and resurrection. The Son of God puts His seal on the promises of the covenant and, in particular, on His part in the work of salvation. The Father speaks in baptism, but so does the Son, promising to contribute His part in the salvation of the elect. Jesus Christ promises to wash them in His blood.

When dealing with the administration of baptism in general, we saw that baptism "witnesseth and sealeth unto us the washing away of our sins through Jesus Christ." Now a new element is added. In baptism, God the Son not only seals purification from all sin through His blood, but He does more. We read: "incorporating us into the fellowship of His death and resurrection." Holy baptism means incorporation into Christ's death and resurrection. The authors borrowed this expression from the apostle Paul, who says in Romans 6:4, "Therefore we are buried with him by baptism into death: that like as Christ was raised up from the dead by the glory of the Father, even so we also should walk in newness of life."

Baptism means to be buried and resurrected with Christ. This description of baptism is biblical, although it may sound somewhat foreign to us. We are not as familiar with adult baptism by immersion, which was something that occurred in the early Christian church regularly—in fact, most of the time. To understand both this expression of the authors and the words of Paul, we must go back to the time of the early church. Imagine an adult at that time who, through God's grace, was converted from heathenism to Christianity and was about to be baptized. This person, instructed by the Holy Spirit, now longs for the moment when he can be baptized both as a sign and seal of his faith in Christ and as evidence of his incorporation into the Christian church. He experiences what baptism signifies and seals—namely, dying with Christ and then being resurrected with Him. Imagine the person being baptized and standing with the preacher at the bank of the river, surrounded by the congregation. The hour has come. The person to be baptized bids farewell to the world and all of heathendom, giving himself up to die to all that is of the old creature and desiring to live in union and communion with Christ. He is immersed in the water and experiences thereby the fellowship of Christ's atoning death. But then he rises out of the water and experiences the fellowship of Christ's acquitting resurrection. As a new man, a Christian, he rises out of the water. "Old things are passed away; behold, all things are become new." Baptism is the definite farewell to the old life and the beginning of a new Christian life.

When we think about Paul's words in this context, we understand what he means when he says, "Therefore we are buried with him by baptism into death: that like as Christ was raised up from the dead by the glory of the Father, even so we also should walk in newness of life." Baptism was a radical departure from the old life and an entrance to the new life. Therefore, when Paul wanted to exhort the Romans to a holy and new Christian walk, he simply had to remind them of their baptism. He wanted to say, "You laid down the old life of sin, did you not? Well then, let your walk be to the honor of God just as Christ was resurrected from the dead to the glory of the Father." Through baptism, the converted heathen received the fellowship of Christ's death and resurrection, and the benefits of Christ's death and resurrection.

The form says, "So that we are freed from all our sins, and accounted righteous before God." The true meaning of baptism gives fellowship with Christ's death and resurrection; Christ's death merited salvation and His resurrection merited deliverance from sin. According to the Word of God, Christ is delivered up for our sins and resurrected for our justification. Those who have communion with Christ and are incorporated into Him through true faith receive these fruits of Christ's death and resurrection.

The guilt of God's church is buried forever in Christ's death and grave. Through His death, God's church is reconciled with God, and, in His resurrection, she is pardoned from all her guilt.

The form says God's people are "accounted" righteous before God. They were condemnable before God through the imputation of Adam's sin, but they are freed from all their sins and accounted righteous before God through the imputation of Christ's death and resurrection. All that Christ performed as Surety is imputed to God's church. What a grace! Sin and guilt are replaced with Christ's satisfaction and obedience. These blessings and fruits of Christ's death and resurrection are sealed in baptism by God the Son. Like the Father, God the Son seals this covenant promise to believers—and not only to all believers, but also to their children. God seals His covenant to the visible church.

In circumcision, God sealed the covenant promise to the whole nation of Israel. In baptism, He does the same for the visible church. But, in all this, election must have its place. There are two kinds of covenant children, for it is not all Israel that is called Israel. When we speak about the position of the children in the church, we start with God's promise of salvation, but we must remember that the essence of the covenant concerns God's elect. We do not know who these are; this is a hidden work of God. In baptism, the Son of God commits Himself to the church and to her seed according to the word spoken to Abraham, "I will be thy God and the God of thy seed." According to God's sovereign good pleasure, these promises of God the Son are fulfilled only to the elect. In the sacraments, God's promises are sealed, but God works what He commands in the elect only. God will work in the elect all that is necessary for them to obtain the benefits of Christ—namely, "incorporating us into the fellowship of his death and resurrection, so that we are freed from all our sins, and accounted righteous before God."

Christ's benefits can never be received without true union with Christ. Only when we are incorporated into Christ, through regeneration and faith, are we freed from our sins and accounted righteous before God. This incorporation into Christ does not come about through the power of our own will or mind; it is the work of God, not man.

We do not receive the salvation merited by Christ just because of the sacrament. This is the teaching of Roman Catholicism, where the sacrament administers grace. The Reformed viewpoint is opposed to this. As the Mediator, Christ not only merits, but also applies. He grants and He applies. Therefore, Reformed theologians have always spoken of the blood and the Spirit of Christ in one thought. The salvation made possible on the cross is applied by the Holy Spirit, and the Holy Spirit is also the Spirit of Christ. Christ makes us partakers of His benefits by incorporating us into His fellowship; this is the only way we receive the benefits of His death and resurrection. From that fellowship with Christ, all blessings flow.

In baptism, God the Son promises to perform this work. He will incorporate sinners into the fellowship of His death and resurrection so that they "are freed from all their sins and accounted righteous before God." Baptism is full of Christ and of His work. Through the Mediator, the covenant is ordered and sure. The Son of God will fulfill His part of the covenant, sealing this to us and our children. According to the hidden counsel of God, the elect will obtain it, but baptism reveals salvation through Christ and opens the covenant in Christ to us. The Son fixes His seal to the promises. He will fulfill His promises in the seed of the church, revealing Himself to sinners as a complete Savior. Thus, through baptism, He admonishes and invites us to seek salvation by none other than Himself. Should not our response to God the Son be the same as David's response to God, "O Lord, do as thou hast said" (2 Sam. 7:25)?

Concerning God the Holy Spirit

Now the Holy Spirit is speaking. The three divine Persons are united in perfect harmony to work out the salvation of the church. In holy baptism, however, the Holy Spirit testifies the strongest. He not only seals His promises, as the Father and the Son do, but He is the Sealer Himself.

What does the Holy Spirit communicate in holy baptism? The form says, "In like manner, when we are baptized in the name of the Holy Ghost, the Holy Ghost assures us, by this holy sacrament, that he will dwell in us, and sanctify us to be members of Christ, applying unto us, that which we have in Christ, namely, the washing away of sins, and the daily renewing of our lives, till we finally shall be presented without spot or wrinkle among the assembly of the elect in life eternal."

From eternity, the Holy Spirit has taken upon Himself the applying of the benefits merited by Christ to sinners. His work is to make dead sinners alive and to work in them a true faith by which they become partakers of the benefits of the covenant. It is this work of the Holy Spirit that we will now discuss. It is the

Holy Spirit Himself who speaks of it in baptism, assuring us that He will perform His part in the saving of the elect.

The first promise of the Holy Spirit to God's church is "that he will dwell in us and sanctify us to be members of Christ."

First, we note that most versions of our form for the administration of baptism read, "dwell with us." However, this is an error introduced by the publishers. The original form reads, "dwell in us." This is the special office of the Holy Spirit.

The Father is God above us and the Son is God for us; however, the Holy Spirit is God in us. In baptism, the Holy Spirit promises to dwell in us as in a temple. This is the content of God's promise in Ezekiel 37:14: "And I shall put my spirit in you, and ye shall live."

The form speaks of the indwelling of the Holy Spirit. On the day of Pentecost, the Spirit came to dwell permanently with, and in, the church on earth. But here we are speaking of the personal indwelling of the Holy Spirit. This is His wondrous work—that He lives in the hearts of sinners. The divine Dove has found His nest in the hearts of men—hearts that by nature are the dwelling place of Satan, where Satan had his blacksmith's shop and forged his evil plans. The Holy Spirit desires to dwell here; how great a blessing this is! It was a great mercy that the Son of God, who dwelt in the company of the angels, chose to live among fallen man and to assume our human nature. Likewise, the love of the Holy Spirit is manifested in this: that He not only dwells *among* man, but also *in* man.

In creation, the Spirit of God moved upon the face of the waters. He ordered creation and gave form where there was no form. In re-creation, the same Spirit descends to renew the heart of man and to re-create it after the image of God.

What exactly does the Spirit do in the heart of man? The form says: "and sanctify us to be members of Christ." As the Son, the Head of the church, promised to suffer and to die in the place of His people, so the Holy Spirit promises to sanctify those for whom Christ died and to make them members of Jesus Christ. From eternity, the elect are included in Christ their

Head, but they are simply represented. The Holy Spirit promises in baptism that, through His work of regeneration and faith, He will make them actual members of Christ.

Union with Christ through faith is very important throughout Scripture. Christ is the Head of the church and the true believers are the members of His body. Union with Him is the only way to partake of His benefits. It is impossible to do so otherwise. We must first be united with Christ through regeneration and faith.

In holy baptism, the Holy Spirit promises to unite God's people with Christ. He will "sanctify" us to be members of Christ. To sanctify means to set apart. The original word carries the connotation of "to cut" or "to cut off." The Holy Spirit cuts sinners off from the old stock of Adam and engrafts them into the true Vine, Jesus Christ. He cuts them off from the old life and sanctifies them. He liberates sinners from the power of Satan and of sin, and engrafts them into Christ.

Before their salvation, the elect are dead in sins and trespasses, as all members of Adam's descendants. They cannot convert themselves, and neither do they want to. By themselves, they cannot believe in Christ nor apply His merited benefits to themselves. Only the Spirit can make dead sinners alive and apply to them the benefits of Christ's death and resurrection. To that end, the Holy Spirit sanctifies them. Those who are baptized are already set apart from among the fallen race of Adam; but the setting apart by the Holy Spirit, who calls and converts from the multitude of lost sinners, far exceeds the setting apart in baptism.

How great is the love of the Holy Ghost in conversion, to sanctify sinners from the mass of fallen man and to engraft them into Christ! God's children are separated, called, and sanctified from the mass of mankind, and they are engrafted into Christ. How blessed is this work! What free grace to call a sinner, who is as guilty as all others, to be united with Christ.

The authors go on to say of the work of the Holy Spirit, "applying unto us, that which we have in Christ." The Lord

Jesus said of the Comforter, the Holy Spirit, "He shall glorify me: for he shall receive of mine, and shall shew it unto you" (John 16:14). Christ is given to the church for wisdom, righteousness, sanctification, and full redemption. In Him, their salvation is complete and nothing can be added to it or taken from it. The Holy Spirit applies Christ's blessings to sinners. He adds nothing to Christ's work, but He applies it all to them.

Lord's Day 20 of the Heidelberg Catechism says concerning the Holy Spirit, "He is also given me, to make me by a true faith, partaker of Christ and all his benefits, that he may comfort me and abide with me for ever." The Spirit applies the benefits of Christ to sinners by granting faith through which we accept Christ, our Righteousness before God. Therefore, the Holy Spirit is also called the Spirit of faith (2 Cor. 4:13). In baptism, He comes to us with this special promise that He will apply what God's elect already have in Christ. This work is not accredited to the person being baptized, but to the Holy Spirit. The form does not speak of "applying unto oneself" what Christ has merited, but of the Holy Spirit applying these benefits to us; the focus is not on the person being baptized, but on the Spirit. Many limit baptism to an offer of Christ and His benefits, leaving the application of Christ's merits entirely to the work of man. But it is the Holy Spirit who applies to us the merits of Christ. Only He makes us possessors of Christ and of all His benefits.

The language of the form distinguishes between the right to ownership and actual ownership. The Spirit makes us partakers of what we already have in Christ; we can view this "have" as meaning "that which Christ promised in baptism." In this case, the emphasis falls on the Holy Spirit applying the promise made in baptism to the church and to her seed. He then gives the promised salvation for possession. Thus it is a promise of future blessing.

In accord with God's sovereignty, this does not apply automatically to each baptized person. However, the Holy Spirit will fulfill the promise made in baptism to the church and her seed. Although Esau despised the blessing, Jacob accepted the promised mercy of the covenant. This is a rich comfort: if the parents had to apply the promise to their baptized children, it would be a miserable and hopeless situation. But the Holy Spirit fulfills the promises that God makes at baptism; this becomes manifest later in the lives of God's people.

With the words "that which we have in Christ," we think of what is already the portion of the elect in the covenant of grace. In Christ, the church possesses everything necessary for life and salvation. In Him, they are included in the eternal covenant of grace and thus they are sanctified, justified, and cleansed from all sin. But to actually obtain possession of this through faith is a work of the Holy Spirit. He promises to apply the benefits they already have in Him, their representative covenant Head, through faith, "namely, the washing away of our sins, and the daily renewing of our lives, till we finally shall be presented without spot or wrinkle among the assembly of the elect in life eternal."

Three benefits are listed here: justification, sanctification, and glorification. When baptism takes place and water flows onto the forehead of the infant or adult, the purifying power of Jesus' blood is visibly preached. The Holy Spirit assures the convicted sinner that as assuredly as the child is washed with water, so he is washed of his sins through Christ's blood. God will fulfill the promise, "Then will I sprinkle clean water upon you, and ye shall be clean: from all your filthiness, and from all your idols, will I cleanse you" (Ezek. 36:25).

A further promise of the Holy Ghost to the church of Christ is "the daily renewing of our lives." The Holy Spirit is the great Renewer; in regeneration, He renews man entirely. This is said so beautifully in the Canons of Dort: "He opens the closed, and softens the hardened heart, and circumcises that which was uncircumcised, infuses new qualities into the will, which though heretofore dead, he quickens; from being evil, disobedient, and refractory, he renders it good, obedient and pliable" (Head III-IV, Article 11).

The Holy Spirit works this blessed work in the hearts of sinners when He regenerates them. His work is glorious and divine, and more powerful than the creation of the world. It is a work for which He shall receive the glory eternally. But, however beautiful this work may be, if the Spirit would leave us to ourselves, what would remain of the work of God in the heart of sinners? Therefore, the form says that the Holy Spirit renews us *daily*. Every day He is the driving force behind the new life. Without His daily influence, there would be no growth or fruit in spiritual life. Without the blowing of wind, the most beautiful organ gives no sound when the keys are touched, but when wind is blown through the bellows, the organ produces beautiful music. Similarly, spiritual life is dependent on a daily renewing by the Holy Spirit. The work of conversion is continued through a daily conversion; God's children are never finished with their conversion.

This is why the form speaks of the conversion of the converted. A daily conversion is essential for them as a continual purging of the old leaven is for a pure lump. Believers feel humbled when God says that believers need *daily* conversion. The word of Jesus to Simon Peter was also humbling: "And when thou art converted, strengthen thy brethren" (Luke 22:32). After they have gone astray, the Holy Spirit converts, as it were, the converted. It is due to His work alone that they return to God after their wanderings. Psalm 51 was penned after David had sinned, and Simon Peter wept bitterly after his denial; these were the works of the Spirit who seals and promises with an oath in baptism to daily renew God's children.

This promise is so precious! The promise of the covenant of grace from Ezekiel 36:27 is sealed in baptism: "And I will put my spirit within you, and cause you to walk in my statutes, and ye shall keep my judgments, and do them."

Because of the knowledge of their sinful selves, true believers would not dare to promise the Lord what Simon Peter did: "I will lay down my life for thy sake." God's exercised people have learned to distrust themselves. Their own heart has deceived them so often that they hesitate to promise anything.

However, the Holy Spirit promises to work in them what they cannot do themselves; He promises a "daily renewing of our lives," and He also promises to continue this work "till we shall finally be presented without spot or wrinkle among the assembly of the elect in life eternal." The Holy Spirit is the Comforter who, according to the word of Jesus, shall remain with the church eternally. He will complete the work of grace in each believer until the whole congregation of God's elect is presented spotless to Christ, her Husband. The Holy Spirit seals in baptism that He will continue His work in all the elect of God until they are brought safely into heaven.

Thus, baptism does not only seal to the church Christ's benefits, but also life eternal. The church of God has an eternal inheritance. The Holy Spirit has taken upon Himself to lead the children of God to glory.

The expression "assembly of the elect" comes from Hebrews 12:23 where the apostle says, "To the general assembly and church of the firstborn, which are written in heaven." Here below, God's visible church is like a fishing net in which good and evil fish have been gathered. It is like a field with wheat and tares. But heaven is an assembly of the elect only. The Holy Spirit promises in baptism to bring all God's people safely to heaven.

"Till we shall finally": this points to a battle that first must be fought and to oppression that first must be suffered. The victorious Holy Spirit will make believers enter into the assembly of God's elect at last in heaven, despite their struggles and all their enemies. His work and labor provides a place in the heavenly Jerusalem for those who are purchased with Christ's blood. His work will be finished when He has presented them spotless before God.

The final destiny is "an assembly of the elect." Out of all nations, kindred, people, and tongues, the Holy Spirit will gather a church, elect unto eternal life. Everything leads to this end—a new mankind with its only Head, Jesus Christ. The covenant will then be fully realized, and God will be all and in all. In eternity the covenant will be unveiled in its full perfection:

God with His people and His people with their God. The Lord will be a God to them and they will be His people.

This is the end of the second part of the form for the administration of baptism and the end of the doctrine of deliverance.

Gratitude

We now have arrived at the third part of the doctrine of holy baptism: the doctrine concerning our gratitude to God. Remember that the form began with saying: "The principal parts of the doctrine of holy baptism are these three." The sprinkled water of baptism first speaks of our misery and curse, and then it testifies of purification and reconciliation. The doctrine of baptism next speaks of gratitude.

A biblical order is followed here as we find in all of our Reformed writings. Just think of the Heidelberg Catechism. Let us be watchful to maintain this order: knowledge of our misery is necessary first, then knowledge of deliverance through Christ, and finally, a call for gratitude. Regarding this third part, the form continues:

> Whereas in all covenants, there are contained two parts: therefore are we by God through baptism, admonished of, and obliged unto new obedience, namely, that we cleave to this one God, Father, Son, and Holy Ghost; that we trust in him, and love him with all our hearts, with all our souls, with all our mind, and with all our strength; that we forsake the world, crucify our old nature, and walk in a new and holy life. And if we sometimes through weakness fall into sin, we must not therefore despair of God's mercy, nor continue in sin, since baptism is a seal and undoubted testimony, that we have an eternal covenant of grace with God.

We must first point out that two words of this version differ from the previous version, which had been used for three centuries. The last line reads, "that we have an eternal covenant of grace with God." The printers have added the words "of grace." This is not actually incorrect, but these words did not appear in the original text.

A covenant always contains two parts, since it is an agreement between two parties. There must be two parties for a covenant to be established. There were two parties in the covenant of works: God and man. There are also two parties in the covenant of grace: God and the sinner.

The wording of the old form makes this clear. There we read, "Whereas in all covenants both parties commit themselves to each other, so also we promise God the Father, Son, and Holy Ghost, that through his grace we will acknowledge him only for our one, true, and living God" (Barger, *Our Church Manual*, p. 210).

In the preceding part, we considered what the first party does. We heard God the Father, Son, and Holy Spirit speak and promise. The covenant of grace is established from only one side—from God's side, not from man's side. God the Father elects to salvation, the Son merits salvation, and the Holy Spirit applies salvation. However, after it has been established, it becomes two-sided when man is admonished to obedience. The form says: "we are admonished of, and obliged unto new obedience." Notice that even *after* the one-sided establishing of the covenant, it is God who determines what our duties are.

God does not only establish the covenant, but He also stipulates the duties for the other party. Yet there appears to be a difficulty here. The two parties in the covenant of grace are God and Christ, the Head of the elect. Several places in Scripture show us that there is a counsel of peace between the Father and the Son. We read in Zechariah 6:13, "And the counsel of peace shall be between them both." Then how can it be established between God and a sinner?

We must remember that the form for the administration of baptism speaks of the administration of the covenant of grace in time. God brings the elect into a covenant with Himself. He establishes the covenant with them in their conversion. Therefore, we do not need to separate the covenant of grace from election and the eternal counsel of peace between the Father and the Son.

In essence, the covenant of grace is the historical perform-ance and realization of election. Election is made visible on earth through the covenant of grace. "The covenant of grace, which is established in time and is propagated from generation unto generation, is nothing else but the image and performance of that covenant that lies firm in the eternal essence of God Himself" (Herman Bavinck, *Magnalia Dei*, p. 265).

The essence of the covenant made in eternity between the Father and the Son and that of the covenant of grace that is per-formed in time is the same—namely, to bring an assembly of elect sinners into communion with God through Christ and the work of the Holy Spirit.

Likewise, Rev. Kersten teaches, when speaking about the execution of the covenant of redemption in time, "Therefore, in order to be saved, each of the elect must actually be taken up into the covenant. They are incorporated into Christ, and thereby made partakers of all His benefits, and brought into covenant relationship with God" (*Reformed Dogmatics*, 1:243).

Concerning the relationship between the covenant of grace in eternity and in time, he continues,

> Just as a person may be described in the testament as the heir or possessor of the goods bequeathed, still, in order to accept it, it must be awarded to him after the death of the testator; yes, just as a prisoner who was acquitted must necessarily have the door opened, and must actually be brought out and set at liberty, so the elect need an actual entrance into the covenant of grace to be saved from their state of misery in which they were conceived and born (ibid.).

The form for the administration of baptism speaks here about the latter point—namely, the actual entrance into covenant with God through faith. In the part concerning redemption, the Father, who made an eternal covenant of grace with the elect, was speaking. Here, in the part of gratitude, the believing sinner comes to the foreground and, through God's grace, accepts and assents to the covenant. The two parts of the covenant are therefore God, who commits Himself to be the

God of His people, and the believing sinner, who commits himself to be one of God's people. Thus, the third part concerns itself with the acceptance of the covenant by the sinner, and this is where the words of the authors become so true: "there are contained two parts."

This covenant proceeds solely and completely from God, and in this respect may be called one-sided. Yet there are in this covenant, as in all covenants, two parts, or two parties: God and the sinner. It is twofold, even though it is God who stipulates and determines everything. By grace, man agrees with all the conditions of the covenant and says "Amen" to it. God says, "I give Myself to you," but He also requires, "Now you must give yourself to Me and no longer serve the devil." By grace, the sinner wholeheartedly agrees to do so.

Calvin explained this by saying, "For as God there promises to cover and efface any guilt and penalty which we may have incurred by transgression, and reconciles us unto himself in his only begotten Son, so we, in our turn, oblige ourselves by this profession to the study of piety and righteousness" (*Institutes*, 4.14).

The sacrament of baptism is a twofold sign—first, of the grace of God toward His church and her seed, and, secondly, of the faith of that church and her seed toward their God. This is also evident in Christ's commandment regarding baptism. First there is the command to baptize, but then He adds, "Teaching them to observe all things whatsoever I have commanded you."

Two parties enter into a true covenant with each other. We are therefore a true partaker of the covenant only when, through saving faith, we have accepted all the conditions of the covenant.

After quoting many verses from Scripture, Wilhelmus à Brakel says, "All these texts clearly confirm that there is a covenant transaction between God and believers, and that it is initiated from God's side by way of proffer and promise, and from the side of man by acceptance and surrender" (*The Christian's Reasonable Service*, 1:431).

We hear God's offer and promises in the second part, where

God the Father, through the sacrament of baptism, testifies and seals to make an eternal covenant of grace with the church and her children. However, this testimony of God in baptism will never be a blessing to us if the covenant is not accepted by way of repentance and faith. Repentance and faith are not conditions on which the realization of the covenant is dependent, but God promises in the covenant of grace to work what He demands. Repentance and faith are held forth to us as the only way through which we can become partakers of God's covenant blessings. The covenant God offers must be accepted by man!

The Acceptance of the Covenant

This third part emphasizes the covenant from the side of the sinner. The sinner has been passive throughout. God was speaking. However, now we hear that baptism "admonishes and obliges unto a new obedience."

Baptism brings all the treasures of God's covenant near us; His promises are sealed on our forehead. In baptism God affixes His seal to the gospel that any man who looks on the crucified Christ and believes in Him shall receive eternal life. The covenant of God, with all its blessings, is offered to us genuinely and freely.

What will happen if we despise such a great salvation? If we refuse to enter into covenant with God, we consider the blood of Christ, which sanctifies, to be unclean, and the dreadful wrath of God will rest on us. The baptized person must therefore give assent to and accept the covenant. So many people say, "You are already a child of God; you already possess the washing away of sins; you only have to remain in this covenant and keep God's laws." They forget that the covenant must be accepted from the side of man in the way of faith and a new obedience.

Reformed theologians, therefore, speak of a sinner assenting to the covenant and of God establishing it. By nature, man is unwilling and incapable of accepting the covenant of God. As Scripture says, man has already made a covenant—a covenant with death and hell. By nature, man is party to a broken covenant of works. Because of sin, we are prisoners of Satan; the strong man keeps us in his power.

Regardless of how clearly and gloriously the covenant is presented, mankind does not naturally want to break with the service of sin for this covenant. By ourselves, we are unwilling to enter into this covenant. The Lord Jesus said, "Ye will not come to me." We are so attached to our idols that we do not want to give them up. The demand of the covenant of God to leave everything and to follow only Christ is too demanding. We are prepared to do much, but we will not leave our favorite sins and sinful desires. Like the sorrowful, rich, young man, we will let Jesus go and maintain our bond with our idols. We say to God, "Depart from us; for we desire not the knowledge of thy ways" (Job 21:14).

Furthermore, by nature, man conducts himself very carelessly in regard to the covenant of grace offered by God in the gospel. He does not see any beauty in it or need for it, and therefore he continues in his unconverted state, saying to himself, "Peace, peace; when there is no peace" (Jer. 6:14).

There is even an aversion to God's covenant in the heart of unregenerate man. The way of the covenant is too narrow for him. Does he really have to leave everything and die to even the very best of his works to be able to enter into that covenant? This is offensive to him. He wants a covenant that allows him to keep his bond with the world; he wants a covenant in which he can keep his good works and religious pride, changing the covenant of grace into a covenant of works. When the method of the covenant is presented to him—a hell-worthy sinner leaving everything in order to be saved—his heart rises up in enmity and is offended at the covenant of God.

The aversion that natural man has against this glorious covenant of grace is indescribable. No sinner would ever enter into that covenant by faith if all the demands of this covenant were not promises as well. In this covenant, God demands repentance and faith, but He also promises that repentance to God and faith in Christ Jesus.

The Bible is full of these promises. Just think of Ezekiel 11:19: "And I will take the stony heart out of their flesh, and will give them an heart of flesh." Through the regenerating work of the Holy Spirit, this takes place in the lives of God's people. The stony heart becomes a heart of flesh. The inborn hatred against God and His covenant is removed from the heart, and a new spirit is received in the inner man. What was previously a burden now becomes a delight. The sinner wants to enter into a covenant with God and to break covenant with Satan, sin, and the world. He desires to commit himself to God and His service.

In conversion, one bond is broken and another bond is formed. The sinner cries out to the world, sin, and Satan, "Get thee hence!"; and he says to God and His service, "A day in thy courts is better than a thousand elsewhere."

Where God's Spirit works in the heart of man, the sinner will break the covenant with death and the agreement with hell. He will renounce the service of the world and give a bill of divorce to sin. With repentance and contrition, he will part from his previous evil lusts and cry out, "Get thee hence, get thee hence!" He will choose, "As for me and my house, we will serve the LORD." He will no longer halt between two opinions, but will cry out, "Now it is in mine heart to make a covenant with the LORD God of Israel" (2 Chr. 29:10).

Man is brought to *accept* God's covenant. The soul does this, according to the answer in Abraham Hellenbroek's catechism, "Calmly, willingly, humbly, faithfully, uprightly, fully agreeing with the demands as well as the promises of the covenant" (*A Specimen of Divine Truths*, p. 37).

The sinner does it "calmly." This means thoughtfully. The costs have been considered in advance. With an enlightened mind, the sinner considers the vanity of the world and the preciousness of the covenant of God. In a reasonable manner, he is convinced and, after thoughtful consideration, submits himself to God's covenant. It does not normally happen the way mass meetings would have it, where people choose Jesus under the impression and emotions of the moment, but rather the choice of God and His service comes from the depths of the heart after struggling with the old life.

The sinner does it "willingly." He does not need to be forced. God's people are willing in the day of His power. In the covenant dealings with God, the sinner has a heartfelt delight in God's covenant. The soul feels inclined to leave Satan and the world forever. He does not leave all his previous lusts because he is forced, but because he neither can, nor will, do otherwise. For such a person, it is impossible to strive and to sin against God any longer; he cannot and does not want to do anything other than join the precious service of the triune covenant God.

The sinner does it "humbly." The sinner who assents to God's covenant finds himself to be in a humble and lowly state. It cannot be described in words how small, poor, and insignificant he discovers himself to be. Like Ezra, he is ashamed and blushes to lift up his face to God. With the penitent publican, he stands afar off because of his sins. He is not worthy that God should come under his roof. Yes, his poverty and insignificance are so great that, because of his sins, he would never dare to enter into a covenant with God if the covenant God Himself had not invited him.

When assenting to the covenant, the covenant God is willing to take away all objections of such a deeply humbled sinner. If the sinner says, "I am not worthy that Thou shouldest come under my roof," then the Lord declares to him, "I do not do it for your sake." If the sinner says, "I am too guilty and I fear for the demands of Thy righteousness," then the Lord says, "Though your sins be as scarlet, they shall be as white as snow." When the sinner says, "I am too unclean because of sin," then the Lord says, "I will sprinkle clean water upon you, and you will be clean from all your filthiness." Against all objections, the Lord sets before the sinner's eyes the riches and glory of Jesus Christ, the Mediator of the covenant. Jesus shows Himself to sinners in the gospel in the fullness of all His merits and offers them gold for their poverty, salve for their blindness, and white raiment for their nakedness. When the sinner says, "I am incapable of fulfilling the demands of the covenant and I do not dare to make an oath that I will never depart from Thy ways," then the Lord replies, "I will make you walk in My precepts and keep My judgments." But, if the sinner then says, "I fear that I will continue to break the covenant and be unfaithful," then the Lord says that He knew from eternity that he would deal unfaithfully with the Lord, but, nevertheless, He will not turn from that sinner. All his unfaithfulness will never nullify the Lord's faithfulness.

The sinner does it "faithfully." The sinner not only sees his misery and condemned state before a holy God, but God also gives him eyes to gaze on the Lord Jesus in His riches and willingness to save such sinners. With all his guilt the sinner believingly turns to the Name of the Lord, who is such a strong tower, thereby professing that God is faithful. As a guilty sinner, he relies on God's promise.

The sinner does it "uprightly and sincerely." He opens his heart to an all-knowing God. Although he knows that he has a deceitful heart, he also knows that he does not deceive himself, because he desires nothing but to enter into an eternal covenant with God.

The sinner does it "fully agreeing with the demands as well as the promises of the covenant." He has no further conditions. He is fully pleased with both the covenant and its Mediator. To sinners like this, the demands of the covenant are as precious as its promises. They love Jesus' commandments as much as His promises.

Thus, the sinner ultimately has nothing left but to surrender himself as a poor sinner in need to the covenant God. He joins with all who say, "We come unto Thee, for Thou art the Lord our God."

Two parties thus truly commit themselves to each other. The sinner relies entirely on God's covenant of grace. He surrenders himself the way he is, and, because of the blood of the Mediator of the covenant, God will wonderfully receive him just as he is, making an eternal covenant with him, giving him the sure mercies of David. The words of à Brakel, whom we quoted before, become genuine reality: that God, in His covenant dealings, commits Himself by proffering and promising, and the sinner commits himself by assenting and surrendering. Then 2 Chronicles 15:12 takes place: "And they entered into a covenant to seek the LORD God of their fathers with all their heart and with all their soul."

We have discussed in depth the first sentence of the third part: "Thirdly. Whereas in all covenants, there are contained two parts." We thought it useful and necessary to point out the necessity of assenting to the covenant in order that there would be no boasting of having a covenant with God without ever having assented to this covenant. Furthermore, the little ones in grace may now examine themselves whether they have exercised true dealings with the triune covenant God, and baptized children are urged to enter into a covenant with God with true repentance and faith in Jesus Christ.

Now we shall proceed and give our attention to the other matters taught us in the third part.

A New Obedience

Therefore are we by God through baptism, admonished of, and obliged unto new obedience.

God has promised to renew His people daily through His Holy Spirit. In turn, having entered into a covenant with God, they are required to walk in a new obedience. "Admonished of, and obliged unto"—so says the form. The theme of the form has changed now to speak of admonition. The theme of the second part was that something is testified and sealed to us. "Sealed" implies that something is given; "admonished" implies that something is required.

So, God requires something of His people in baptism. He admonishes them of and obliges them to new obedience. He not only admonishes, saying, "You ought to do it!" but He also obliges, which means, "I demand it from you!" What does God demand? God demands a "new obedience."

This "new" obedience contrasts with an "old" obedience. It contrasts with the previous lives of the believers, when they obeyed Satan and sin. However, now they are called to a new obedience. "Old things are passed away; behold, all things are become new" (2 Cor. 5:17).

What is this new obedience? You will find the answer in the form: "namely, that we cleave to this one God, Father, Son, and Holy Ghost; that we trust in him, and love him with all our hearts, with all our souls, with all our mind, and with all our strength." Love is the fulfillment of the law. God wants His people to obey Him out of love. The law of love is how the law applies in the life of gratitude.

Above the law is now written, "I am the LORD thy God." The law no longer belongs to the covenant of works, but to the covenant of grace; it is the same law, but employed in a different manner. This time the law urges obedience—not in a condemning manner, but in a most loving and evangelical manner. In this third part, the law comes to God's church in an evangelical covenant form. It does not say, "Do this or you will be cursed," but rather, "You are bought with a price: therefore glorify God in your body, and in your spirit." No longer is the motive, "Otherwise I will be cursed," but "Otherwise I will grieve God."

The threatening here is different from that of the covenant of works, which says, "I will condemn you if you do not keep My law." Now it is, "I will hide My countenance from you." In a life of gratitude, God's children do not fear condemnation, for Christ has borne that for them. Someone with a slavish fear only keeps God's law to escape hell. However, someone with a child-like fear says, "Otherwise God will hide His kindly face and I will grieve my God." It is an evangelical motive that makes God's children to call out, "O that my ways were directed to keep thy statutes!" (Ps. 119:5). The cords of love draw them to their duties. This is the motive with which God approaches His church in baptism. It concerns cleaving, trusting, and loving with all our hearts.

Love is the motive behind gratitude—love to the God who seals to His people in baptism that He will grant them everything necessary for their salvation. Love is required toward the Father, who elected them in Christ, and who adopted them for His sons and daughters. Love is required toward the Son, who redeemed them from their guilt and punishment, so that they are delivered from all their sins. Love is required toward the Holy Spirit, who made His abode in their hearts and sanctified them to be members of Christ. In summary, love is required toward the triune covenant God, who is a God of full salvation for His people.

The requirement Jesus gave is this: "Love the Lord thy God with all thy heart, and with all thy soul, with all thy mind, and with all thy strength" (Mark 12:30). God lays a claim on the entire person. He is not satisfied with only a part of our lives. First, He demands our entire heart, for "out of it are the issues of life" (Prov. 4:23). Second, He demands our entire soul; Calvin says of the soul, "It is the origin of all affections." God claims our affections for Himself. Third, He demands our entire mind. Our reason is the ability to accept or reject something, to esteem something highly or to despise it. God claims this ability for Himself. Fourth, He demands all our strength. He requires that all our strength be used to increase His glory.

When the sinner agreed to this covenant, he gave himself over entirely to the covenant God. That is why the covenant God claims the entire person for Himself from then on. Love summarizes the first commandment, "Thou shalt have no other gods before me." Nothing else and no one else shall be your god.

That we forsake the world, crucify our old nature, and walk in a new and holy life.

Baptism says, "Leave the world!" The water of baptism speaks of separation. In the early Christian churches, it was customary that before being immersed in the water of baptism, the new convert would, with his face turned toward the east, say farewell to Satan and the world. Having done this, he would then receive the mark and sign of Christianity and be obliged to walk in a new and holy life. To be baptized meant to be separated from this evil world.

The world is the kingdom of sin. God does not demand that we lock ourselves away in a monastery; yet, although we are *in* the world, we ought not to be *of* the world.

Baptism is a mark and sign of our belonging to Christ. This does not mean that we sit somewhere in a corner and muse about the evil world, but it means that we show in our conduct who we serve and to whom we belong.

"Crucify our old nature." Man must not only break with sin outwardly, but also inwardly. He must not only behave differently, but also be and remain different.

The old nature is the name for the remnants of the sinful man that cleave to believers. This old nature must be mortified, for it cannot be healed or made better in this life. It must be crucified. Just as in circumcision in Israel the foreskin was thrown away, so the old man must be cut off and thrown away. The cross of the Lord Jesus is not only an object on which Christ was crucified and on which He satisfied for sin, but it is also the instrument on which believers die. Does the apostle not say, "I am crucified with Christ?" Without the cross, Jesus would not be Jesus. Likewise, without the crucifixion of his evil nature a Christian would not be a Christian.

The cross of Christ mortifies our evil nature. From Jesus, the crucified One, flow two results. First, our sins were imputed to Him on the cross so that God will no more remember them and, secondly, our old nature is nailed on the cross to die the slow, painful, and grievous death of crucifixion. Many boast in the cross of Christ as the place where Jesus died, but they do not want to die on it themselves. The knowledge of the love of Christ, shown on the cross, mortifies the old man. It makes sin more bitter than anything else.

"And walk in a new and holy life." The result of sanctification is a new and holy life. Godliness, in essence, means living a life with God, like that of Enoch. Enoch walked with God and after God. He fulfilled what was written later in the letter to the Ephesians, "Be ye therefore followers of God, as dear children" (5:1). A true Christian must resemble Christ his Master. He must think as Christ did. He must live as Christ lived. That is real godliness. Oh, how ashamed we should be of ourselves that we have so little of the image of the great Example.

May the Lord make us cleave to Him; the more we are united with Him, the more His virtues will become part of us. The branch cannot bear fruit when it does not remain in the Vine.

This concludes the admonition of the sacrament of baptism.

An Eternal Covenant

And if we sometimes through weakness fall into sin, we must not therefore despair of God's mercy, nor continue in sin, since baptism is a seal and undoubted testimony, that we have an eternal covenant of grace with God.

Our Reformed fathers knew that believers will not obtain perfection in this life. They knew all too well that God's children remain imperfect, sinful people here below. Anyone who thinks that believers can come so far in holiness that they never sin anymore will find Scripture against them. John writes that we deceive ourselves when we say we have no sin (1 John 1:8) and James says, "For in many things we offend all" (3:2). Our lives show the inner corruption of our nature. However, a regenerate person will not use the knowledge of remaining corruption of the flesh as an excuse for his daily stumbling. Sin is his sorrow and grief. The life of grace in the soul can never live with sin in peace; the renewed heart desires to serve God and says, "I wish that all sin in me were dead."

Therefore, here in the form we are considering "falling into sin through weakness"—not living in sin, but falling into sin. A true partaker of the covenant can never live in sin. However,

David, Peter, and others are proofs of the weakness present in even the most faithful.

God's children can fall. Sinful things can tempt them so much that they fall. But when they sin, baptism reminds them that they do not need to despair. They may break the covenant from their side, but God will never break it from His side. They may seriously grieve the Bridegroom through sin, but He will never give them a bill of divorce. The comfort of the covenant is not annulled through their weakness.

When God's children fall, Satan tries to make them despair of God's grace. This has always been his abominable work. He first tempts them to sin, and afterwards he tries to bring them to despair because of their sin. In their hearts, they may despair of the very grace of God. Wandering from God's paths suppresses their boldness in faith. They grieve the Holy Spirit and reject His comforting dealings, and the consequences are darkness, assaults of Satan, and fear. The form has these bitter fruits of sin in view when it says: "And if we sometimes through weakness fall into sin, we must not therefore despair of God's mercy."

"Despair," says the form. This is different from doubting. The devil whispers to the despairing ones, "You are finished forever. There is no more grace for someone like you." The question may arise in their hearts whether they have sinned away the grace of God and whether God has withdrawn Himself for good. This temptation is a bitter fruit of sin that also can harbor a great danger; the authors saw that this despairing of God's grace harbors the danger of remaining in sin. He who gives up all hope of grace is in danger of saying, "Now it is a lost case!" He will make no attempt to return to God. The form warns us against this temptation of Satan. The thought that there is no more grace is not of God, but of Satan.

Our sins *are* contrary to the love required of us by the covenant, but this does not mean that, after repentance, God will no longer remember His covenant. To the contrary, the grace of God is sufficient to blot out all sin. When God in grace inclines Himself toward His people, who He loves, it is not a superficial emotional impulse, but an eternal one. Amid the temptation, the covenant of grace is a comfort. God's grace and forgiveness are always available, even after we have fallen deeply into sin.

If we repent and return to God, the grace of God is sufficient to blot out all sin. Baptism reminds those who are fallen into such depths "that we have an eternal covenant with God." The believer does not need to think, "My punishment is greater than I can bear." No, the sacrament of baptism reminds him, "Even if you have 'played the harlot with many lovers, yet return again to me'" (Jer. 3:1). This call to return proceeds from the covenant of grace. God always called Israel to return to Him in this way: "Turn, O backsliding children...for I am married unto you" (Jer. 3:14). The breach is from our side, never from God's side. God says in baptism, "You let me go, but I will never let you go."

God made a covenant with His people. "For the mountains shall depart, and the hills be removed; but my kindness shall not depart from thee, neither shall the covenant of my peace be removed" (Isa. 54:10). How gloriously the faithfulness of God's covenant shines to those who, because of weakness, fall into sin.

We agree with Calvin, who says so beautifully, "Therefore, as often as we fall away, we ought to recall the memory of our baptism and fortify our mind with it, that we may always be sure and confident of the forgiveness of sins" (*Institutes*, 4.15.3).

Of course, this doctrine may not be used in an antinomian way: "Let us 'continue in sin, that grace may abound'" (Rom. 6:1). In this context, Calvin says further, "Rather, this doctrine is only given to sinners who groan, wearied and oppressed by their own sins, in order that they may have something to lift them up and comfort them, so as not to plunge into confusion and despair" (ibid.). It is evident that this part of the form for the administration of baptism was drafted up in the Paltz with Calvin's help. Baptism retains its power even after the water of baptism is dry.

We have now arrived at the source of comfort for those who

stumble and fall through weakness. Such people are greatly comforted by baptism. There is no one who, because of his sin, has to despair of grace. This applies in particular to those who are baptized. Your baptism reminds you, "With Me there is forgiveness, that I may be feared." As often as you stumble, remember that you have an eternal covenant with God. When we are unfaithful, He remains faithful.

This makes those of us who stumble say with David, "Although my house be not so with God; yet he hath made with me an everlasting covenant, ordered in all things, and sure: for this is all my salvation, and all my desire" (2 Sam. 23:5).

The Lord calls to His church, "My covenant will I not break...nor suffer my faithfulness to fail" (Ps. 89:34, 33).

CHAPTER 2

The Doctrine of
Infant Baptism in Particular

We will now deal with an entirely different part of the form for the administration of baptism. Having dealt with the doctrine of baptism in general, the form now deals with the doctrine of infant baptism in particular.

> And although our young children do not understand these things, we may not therefore exclude them from baptism, for as they are without their knowledge, partakers of the condemnation in Adam, so are they again received unto grace in Christ; as God speaketh unto Abraham, the father of all the faithful, and therefore unto us and unto our children, saying, "I will establish my covenant between me and thee, and thy seed after thee, in their generations, for an everlasting covenant; to be a God unto thee, and to thy seed after thee." This also the Apostle Peter testifieth, with these words, "For the promise is unto you and to your children, and to all that are afar off, even as many as the Lord our God shall call." Therefore God formerly commanded them to be circumcised, which was a seal of the covenant, and of the righteousness of faith; and therefore Christ also embraced them, laid his hands upon them and blessed them. Since then baptism is come in the place of circumcision, therefore infants are to be baptized as heirs of the kingdom of God, and of his covenant. And parents are in duty bound, further to instruct their children herein, when they shall arrive to years of discretion.

The first thing the authors say is: "And although our young children do not understand these things." Our forefathers had to defend the administration of holy baptism to children of the congregation against the Anabaptists in particular, and therefore describe the scriptural basis for infant baptism.

Our Reformed fathers also had to battle the Roman Catholic viewpoint of the sacrament, which teaches that the sacraments are always and unconditionally efficacious, whether one believes or not. The Roman Catholics call the sacraments "vehicles of God's grace." However, according to Scripture, the Reformed viewpoint is that the sacraments can confirm and seal God's grace to us only when they are received in faith. According to Scripture, the Reformed forefathers said that, without faith, the sacraments would not benefit us. The Reformers strongly defended the need for exercising faith to receive comfort through the sacraments; the sacraments comfort us only when they are received in faith. Calvin explains the Reformed viewpoint when he says, "The Holy Ghost works in us not only that we see the sacrament with our eyes, but also that it affects us inwardly."

Calvin did not only use Scripture to refute Rome's teaching. He was very familiar with the old church fathers and quoted them. He often quoted Augustine on the sacraments: "The Word does not work in the sacrament by itself or by the speaking of him who administers it, but by faith which is worked by the Holy Spirit." So Calvin proved that the Reformed viewpoint was not a new viewpoint, but one that had existed from the beginning of the true Christian church.

However, the Anabaptists replied, "If that is true, then infants should not be baptized as they do not have faith." And indeed, this objection seemed to have a solid foundation—at least sufficiently sound to mislead many. It is argued that baptism is a sacrament to strengthen faith, and since a child cannot exercise faith, he may not receive this sacrament. A child of only a few days old does not understand anything about the things that are discussed in the form. He does not understand being conceived and born in sin, and being subject to the wrath of God. He does not understand the washing in the blood of Christ nor the riches of the covenant of grace. Neither does he understand anything of the demands of holy baptism—to walk in a new and holy life. These reasons indeed seem to be sufficient to deny baptism to children.

The Anabaptists even say that to baptize children is to imitate Rome. Rome baptizes inanimate and unconscious things such as churches and bells, and the Protestant church does likewise when it baptizes a child who cannot reason yet and does not understand anything of baptism.

What can we say to this? The authors of the form say, "And although our young children do not understand these things, we may not therefore exclude them from baptism." And why may we not exclude them from baptism? The answer is: "for as they are without their knowledge, partakers of the condemnation in Adam, so are they again received unto grace in Christ."

As a first proof of infant baptism, the two covenant heads, Adam and Christ, are contrasted: the consequences of Adam's breach of the covenant with Christ's obedience. The form began, "That we with our children are conceived and born in sin, and therefore are children of wrath." Because of Adam's fall, the children who have not actually sinned are yet children of wrath because they are in Adam.

The authors say, "Well then, if it is possible to be in Adam because he is our covenant-head, even though the children cannot reason, then according to Scripture it is also possible for infants to be in Christ, even though the children cannot reason or exercise faith." Adam is contrasted with Christ. In Adam, all children are subject to condemnation. His sin is accounted to them. If it is possible that children are accounted children of wrath because of the sin of Adam, is it then impossible that they are accounted righteous in Christ? If children can be subject to condemnation in Adam, without having actually committed any sin, then according to Scripture it is also possible that children can be in Christ without having exercised faith. If the sin of the first Adam extends so far that already by birth his posterity shares in his guilt and depravity, then based on Scripture we profess that the efficacy of the second Adam also extends so far that all His people share in the imputation of His righteousness even *prior* to the use of reason and the exercise of faith. Based on this biblical and covenantal reasoning the authors conclude, "so are they again received unto grace in Christ."

Our condemnation flows forth from the imputation of Adam's sin. A share in grace flows forth from the imputation of Christ's righteousness. If God can righteously impute Adam's sin to children without their knowledge, then it must also follow that God can impute Christ's righteousness to them without their knowledge. This invalidates the teaching that children cannot believe and therefore may not be baptized. According to this reasoning, all children dying at a young age would be condemned. But Scripture teaches that even young children can be recipients of the regenerating working of the Holy Spirit; He is not incapable of working in small children who cannot yet reason or exercise faith. This is clear from the example of John the Baptist who leaped in his mother's womb when Elisabeth was greeted by Mary who carried his Savior in her womb. What is crucial is that God beholds a child in Christ.

Salvation in Christ is founded neither in knowledge nor in the exercising of faith. If this were so, the Lord could not work grace in one who has no knowledge or who is mentally handicapped. We may not limit the Holy Spirit thus. In a manner that is incomprehensible to us, He can do His work in anyone who is without knowledge and in young children. Those who have a sound mind and have come to the years of discretion can be saved only by repentance and faith; but the form applies to young children and those who are mentally handicapped: "without their knowledge."

Therefore, the fact that children have no knowledge cannot be a valid reason for withholding baptism. Our condemnation in Adam does not depend on our knowledge. Likewise, God's acceptance of a sinner in Christ does not depend on our awareness of it.

Needless to say, this part of the form deals with infant baptism and concerns only young children and those without knowledge. But there is another aspect to the teaching of those who hold that only people who have faith may be baptized. If baptism depends on faith, does not the condition for receiving baptism lie in the worthiness of man?

Concerning this issue, Luther says, "The Anabaptists say that a child is not worthy to be baptized, because it does not believe, as if this were a proper conclusion: he is worthy to be baptized who believes and has faith. Does this not mean that God is robbed of what is *His?* For it is only God who baptizes. Therefore, He baptizes not in vain, but He baptizes a sinner, who is unworthy of baptism. Yea, He baptizes a person, who is worthy of condemnation. Therefore, he who does not wish to deceive himself or be mistaken, should not say that he is baptized because he believed, but let him glory in that he is baptized by God's own hands. When you desire to be baptized again you deny that you are baptized by God. God will not leave this sin to remain unpunished because you, oh man, nullify His work, because He has commanded to baptize in His Name."

God has given baptism to us as a sign of His covenant. Our knowing and believing are not the foundation for baptism; the foundation is God's covenant and His promises. Baptism is not administered to the child because of his or her faith or the faith of the parents, but because of faith in God's promises.

Likewise, the children of the Israelites were not circumcised because they had faith, but because God wanted to seal His covenant through circumcision. The child was circumcised because it belonged to those to whom God had given His covenant and promises. So it is with baptism. Our children belong to the visible church to whom God has given His covenant and promises, and therefore we have our children baptized.

The Belgic Confession of Faith says in article 34, "Whom we believe ought to be baptized and sealed with the sign of the covenant, as the children in Israel formerly were circumcised, upon the same promises which are made unto our children." Baptism does not in the first place concern the child or the parents, but God's covenant. It is not the faith of the child that is sealed, but God's promises and covenant. God's covenant and His promises are the basis upon which we have our children baptized.

The form further explains this when it professes, "as God speaketh unto Abraham, the father of all the faithful, and therefore to us and our children."

Abraham and the Congregation
The Lord spoke very clearly to Abraham that His gracious acceptance of Abraham also involved his children. The content of the covenant promise to Abraham was that the Lord would not only be his God, but also the God of his seed after him to a thousand generations. Nowhere does the covenant of grace shine more gloriously than in God's promise to Abraham.

Abraham becomes the father of a new generation, that of the faithful. The apostle Paul calls Abraham "the father of all the faithful." Abraham is a father in two ways. He is the father of a carnal seed of all Israelites and related nations. But, in particular, he is the father of a spiritual seed of all true believers. Paul called the Galatians children of Abraham, even though, according to the flesh, they were not related to Abraham at all. He said, "Know ye therefore that they which are of faith, the same are the children of Abraham" (Gal. 3:7). Throughout the entire letter, and particularly in the third chapter, the apostle teaches the Galatians that, even though they have not one drop of Abraham's blood in their veins, they are yet children of Abraham because they have the same precious faith in Christ as Abraham had.

Later we will elaborate on this distinction between the two kinds of children: those of the flesh and those of the spiritual seed of Abraham.

The Lord said to Abraham, "And I will establish my

covenant between me and thee and thy seed after thee in their generations for an everlasting covenant, to be a God unto thee, and to thy seed after thee." With these words the Lord put Himself in a covenant with Abraham and his descendants. In the Old Testament, the Lord established His covenant first with the patriarchs and later with the people of Israel. In the New Testament, the Lord established His covenant with the visible church, and His covenant is propagated through the generations in the church. This church is like the church of the Old Testament, where it was not all Israel that is called Israel. This church consists of chaff and wheat. Indeed, the true members of the church are a small flock; the majority carries the name of Christian only outwardly.

God, however, has placed His covenant in the community of the visible church just as He placed His covenant in Israel in the Old Testament, the majority of whom died in the wilderness through unbelief. Even though the Old Testament assembly of people lacked much, yet God called it a holy assembly. Likewise, we must not lose sight of the fact that God has placed His covenant in the church, even though it is not a perfect church. He promises to glorify Himself in her and her seed just as He promised to glorify Himself in Israel under the Old Testament. This is what the authors mean with the expression "and therefore unto us and our children."

Our Reformed fathers here profess that the Lord promises us and our children the same promise he gave to Abraham. Thus, baptism also concerns our children. Our fathers saw the line of God's covenant continuing from the Old Testament church to the New Testament church. God placed His covenant in the bosom of the church. God's covenant continues from children unto children and from generation unto generation. Grace is not inheritable, yet it is commonly distributed according to the order of the covenant—in the line of generations. God grants His grace through the generations; He is the God of Abraham, Isaac, and Jacob. It is not vainglory when the Reformers say, "What the Lord said to Abraham He now says to the visible church, to us and our children." History shows that this is true; the wonder of God's covenant is revealed to us again and again. We see the sons in the places of the fathers. God fills the vacant places in the offices, and the empty places among those who fear the Lord are filled from among the children of the visible church.

Those who observe God's works of grace in the visible church will see the fulfillment of the promise, "I will establish my covenant between me and thee and thy seed after thee in their generations for an everlasting covenant, to be a God unto thee, and to thy seed after thee." We dishonor the faithfulness of the Lord in the keeping of His covenant when we complain about times of spiritual poverty. God's work will continue! The reason for this lies in the covenant of which God spoke unto Abraham "and therefore unto us and our children." God is a God of the covenant. He is the God of Abraham, but also the God of Isaac and of Jacob. Therefore, what the Lord promised to Abraham and his seed He also promises to us and our children. This is what the authors profess. God's covenant is more full now than during the Old Testament.

It is appropriate to delve somewhat deeper into this matter. First, we ought not to focus too much upon the child being baptized. We have already emphasized that infant baptism concerns neither the faith nor regeneration of the child, but the covenant and the promises of God. Rev. J. C. Appelius, a man whose orthodoxy is above reproach, covered this matter in detail. Writing about the words: "and therefore unto us and our children," he says, "First we must consider who the persons are for whom infant baptism is a sacrament and seal of the covenant. As for Abraham circumcision was a sacrament of the covenant that God had made with him concerning his seed, so is infant baptism a sacrament and seal not for the child in particular, unto whose body the sacrament is administered, but for the church, with whom God has made His covenant concerning her seed" (*Principle Foundation of the Sacraments*, p. 87). Thus, Appelius states what we concluded from the words of the form—that since God told Abraham and Israel, "I will be a God unto thee, and to thy seed after thee," in the sacrament of baptism He says the same to the church of the New Testament.

Appelius continues, "But the same [the administration of baptism] must be a sacrament for the church, concerning her seed, to strengthen her faith in the covenant which God made with Abraham, as the father of all the faithful, and with the church as her mother. This is the reason why infant baptism is administered in the assembly of the church."

Thus, infant baptism is a seal to the church of the truth of God's covenant. In baptism, God has something to say to the church. Appelius calls the church "the mother" of her seed; Abraham represented the Israelites, but the church represents her children, the children of the visible church. So baptism speaks to the church. God seals to her and to her seed His covenant promises. He promises to build His church out of her and to propagate His Name among her children. His electing love will be revealed in her.

In his explanation of this promise to Abraham, Appelius wants to draw our attention to the church. As the promise of the covenant under the Old Testament rested on Israel, so it now rests on the visible church. In baptism, God promises to build His church from among the seed of the visible church according to His sovereign election, which is anchored in His covenant. Appelius wants to avoid thinking only of the child and his parents when baptism is administered and wants us to think of the church as a whole. God does not seal that every child who receives the seal of the covenant will surely be saved, but He seals His covenant and promises to the whole church. We focus too much on the child that is baptized, and too little on the church among which God visibly seals His covenant on her children's foreheads.

Some have said, "If I knew which children were elected, I would baptize those children only." Clearly, those who say this do not properly understand what baptism is. Holy baptism is not only a sacrament and seal to the child, but to the church. The covenant was not made with Abraham in the believing and elected children, but in all children that received the sign and seal of the covenant. Each circumcised child proclaimed the promise of God made to Abraham. Even when it was not a seal for the child—even when he or she rejected the promise and despised the privileges—it was still a seal for Abraham and his seed. Even if it is not a seal to the child, it remains a seal to the church.

Appelius instructs us here as well. He says, "When all children of the family of Abraham were circumcised then this did not mean that the promise concerned each and every child, for the children of the promise, the election of which God kept for Himself, are counted for the seed (Rom. 9:8). This [circumcision] happened only because Abraham could not know in advance who were the elected children of the covenant in particular; so that he had liberty to plead for all children, be it in subjection to the Lord's counsel, and so that Abraham, receiving the covenant in all the children, would be abundantly strengthened" (ibid., p. 90). This last thought especially deserves our attention.

By sealing the promises of the covenant to each and every child, Abraham and the church obtained abundant strength and had the liberty to plead for the fulfillment of the covenant promises for all children. How far-reaching is the significance of infant baptism! It signifies something for the church, the parent, and the child that is baptized. Every time a child is baptized before the congregation, God calls unto the congregation with an oath, "My truth will stand forever, My covenant-bonds I will not sever."

Holy baptism gives liberty to plead with God for the baptized children. Appelius says, "Baptism provides the church with liberty to come with each child, however evil or wicked it may be, before a holy and righteous God, and to plead for the cleansing of guilt and sin for this child, with full, assured, and trusting confidence that the child will be acceptable with God, and that God's promises and her desire, if not in this child, then in others, will certainly be fulfilled" (ibid., p. 90). How great are the duties of the church and parents! The church receives the sealing of God's covenant in her own seed in order to be spiritually active before God. She need not doubt whether she is welcome by God with this pleading, as God Himself gave His promise to her for that reason. The church, and especially parents, may show God His own seal and promise and pray with liberty, "Do, Lord, as Thou hast spoken."

Not only may the parents and the congregation, but the child, too, may find comfort in the seal of baptism when he or she grows up! Appelius says that the baptized child "may consider that he or she belongs to those children with whom the promise was made and sealed unto the church. Based upon the covenant that God made and sealed unto the church, he or she may come to the Lord with liberty to have that promise made unto the church fulfilled unto himself or herself. The child may be fully assured that when he or she comes thus, that child will be accepted. There is nothing in the child why this should happen. God will do it because of the power of the eternal, unchangeable covenant, which He made with and sealed unto the holy church" (ibid., p. 93).

How this ought to comfort those who are baptized, and how diligently they should be engaged in holy work with it. Even though they find nothing in themselves why God would do it, which is exactly what should be felt in holy wrestling with God, yet there is a ground in baptism that God will do it because of His eternal covenant.

Not without reason, Rev. L.G.C. Ledeboer writes in his well-known question and answer booklet for children that we have to pray for conversion and regeneration. When question 43 asks, "Do we have a warrant for this?," the answer is, "Yes, in our baptism" (*Simple Questions for Children*, p. 5). We are without rights in ourselves; baptism must be the pleading ground for our supplications to God. While grievously confessing that we are children of wrath, having been born and conceived in sin, we may show God our baptized forehead and pray, "Oh Lord, do it for Thy Name's sake."

So Appelius continues, "For this reason, we find so often in the holy Scriptures that the saints, supplicating before the throne of God, plead upon the promises, that have been sworn not unto them only, but also to Abraham and the church" (ibid., p. 95). The ground for baptizing the children of the church lies in God's covenant. The sacraments are the seals of the promise of the covenant, and the promise of the covenant is not for the adults only, because the Lord said unto Abraham, "And unto thy children." The Lord says to the New Testament church as well, "And unto your children" (Acts 2:39). If the promise is for the children, then the sign and seal of that promise is also for them.

Baptism is a sign of the covenant, not of faith; the promise of the covenant is the ground for baptism. With the Anabaptist, the emphasis is on what man does. Baptism for them means that the covenant is accepted from their side; it is a sign of obedience and of following Christ. The emphasis is then on the person being baptized. The faith of the person baptized, and no longer God's covenant and promise, then becomes the ground for baptism.

For the Reformers, baptism was a seal of God! God seals His covenant, and He promises to glorify His covenant throughout all generations. All who object to infant baptism do not rightly understand the covenant of grace. Alexander Comrie, one of the leaders of the Dutch Second Reformation, says,

> It frustrates orthodox ministers greatly when they hear people who argue about baptism. There are some who refuse to read out the questions, others insist that the parents or witnesses are converted—as if baptism was a seal of the faith of the parents or the witnesses, and that especially the children of such converted parents have a right to baptism. Baptism neither seals the subjective faith of the parents, nor a faith in those who are baptized, but only in God's promise—that as all who belong to Adam are condemned in him, so all who belong to Christ, the second Adam, shall be saved through Him. We profess to believe this divine truth in baptism and therefore we have our children baptized. God seals this divine

truth in and through baptism and He fulfils the promise in His time (*Heidelberg Catechism*, pp. 122-123).

What the Lord said unto Israel, He says therefore "unto us and our children." This is further confirmed when the form quotes Peter's testimony on the day of Pentecost.

Peter's Testimony

This also the Apostle Peter testifieth, with these words, "For the promise is unto you and to your children, and to all that are afar off, even as many as the Lord our God shall call" (Acts 2:39).

The authors of the form affirm that, in the New Testament, the Lord says to us and our children what He said earlier to Abraham and Israel. Peter said the same thing on Pentecost when he called to the multitude, "For the promise is unto you and to your children." Peter appealed to the old covenant. The promise mentioned here is the promise of the Holy Spirit and His gifts, as it was promised in Joel 2:28. This was also a promise of the covenant of grace. For this reason, the Dutch annotations say regarding Acts 2:39, "Namely, as previously declared in Joel 2:28, which was according to the covenant of God which He made with Abraham and his seed (Gen. 17:7)." The translators connect Peter's words with Genesis 17:7 as well.

For Peter, the promise concerns God's covenant with Abraham and Israel. Actually, in the original language it says, "The promise is yours." Peter could say this to the Jews because of the covenant God made with their father Abraham according to the flesh.

Peter said to his hearers, "For the promise is unto you." Thomas Boston explains this in the following manner, "Therefore the apostle lays down, for the foundation of faith, to those who had even imbrued their hands in the blood of the Lord of glory, their interest in the promise, Acts 2:39, 'For the promise is unto you, and to your children, and to all that are afar off, even as many as the Lord our God shall call.' To whomsoever then the gospel comes, we may warrantably say the promise is to you, and to you, and every one of you; even the promise of the testament: and ye have access to claim it by faith, as your own legacy, your own mercy" (*Complete Works of Thomas Boston*, 8:540).

Boston even emphasizes that although their hands were defiled with the blood of the Messiah, yet the promise was still given to them. He points out that this is the offer of grace in the gospel, where God offers Christ, clothed in the promises of the gospel, to all who hear His Word. When Peter said, "For the promise is unto you," he gave those who were convicted in their hearts a ground for their faith, as Boston says, offering and showing them the promises of the covenant of grace.

We must not seek grounds for this offer in the fact that Peter's hearers were convicted. When we do that, we lay grounds for the offer of the covenant benefits in man. Such reasoning would not hold, since the apostle added, "And to your children." These children had no knowledge of their sin and therefore were not convicted of sin; yet the benefits of the covenant are offered to them also. No, Peter said this to them for a different reason, as the annotations point out: "Which was according to the covenant of God which He made with Abraham and his seed."

Belonging to the external covenant brings this earnest and genuine offer of the covenant benefits. This is the administration of the covenant of grace: it offers the covenant benefits to all that hear the gospel. God's covenant benefits are not offered to each and every nation, but only to those to whom He sends His gospel according to His good pleasure, to those who live under the administration of the covenant.

Peter did not want the multitude to doubt whether the promises of the covenant were for them. He said, "They are unto you." This means, "You have access to them," or, as Boston says, "Ye have access to claim it by faith, as your own legacy, your own mercy." Peter opened the door to the covenant benefits and said, "For the promise is unto you and to your children." He did not say, "God promised to save all of you and you are all true partakers of the covenant as your father Abraham was." Rather, he said, "For the promise is unto you." You have a holy right of access to the covenant benefits, because God has given His promises to you, the seed of Abraham.

In his preaching at the time of Pentecost, Peter described the privileges of the covenant relationship to the Jews who heard him. In Acts 3:25, he says to them, "Ye are the children of the prophets, and of the covenant which God made with our fathers, saying unto Abraham, and in thy seed shall all the kindreds of the earth be blessed." He always spoke to them of the God of Abraham, Isaac, and Jacob, the God of our fathers (Acts 3:13).

Furthermore, based on that covenant relationship, he called those who crucified the Messiah "brethren." He did not lose sight of the fact that these Jews who rejected Christ were still loved for their father's sake, and that because of this privilege they were called the more earnestly to repentance and faith in Christ. He knew that he did not speak to Gentiles, but to Abraham's seed. Their deeds had been terrible; they had crucified their Messiah. Their hands dripped with the blood of Him who was the One promised to the fathers. But Peter told them that even though they had performed this terrible deed, yet God had not withdrawn His promises to Abraham and his seed; the privileges of that promise still applied. God recognized them as Abraham's descendants, regardless of how guilty they may have been of the blood of the Messiah, and offered them His covenant blessings. But, considering their privilege, this preaching of grace made their rejection of Christ the more heinous. Peter's preaching to them was full of mercy, but he did not want them to doubt divine grace because of their rejection of the Messiah. Therefore he tells them that the grace of the Messiah was especially for them.

"And to your children." The Dutch annotations, commenting on Acts 2:39 say, "That is, your sons and daughters." Here the children are put on the same level as the adults. Did God not speak to Abraham and Israel about their descendants? Peter does likewise and says, "And to your children."

This text is powerful evidence for the support of infant baptism. The Anabaptists do not know what to do with Peter's words; they explain it figuratively and spiritually. Whenever our Reformed fathers confirmed that children were comprehended in the covenant relationship and therefore had a right to the external sign of the covenant, the Anabaptists could not deny it. Ultimately, they explained the quotation, "and to your children" figuratively and spiritually. They said that Peter meant those who are of a childlike spirit, or their spiritual offspring. And this explanation is not uncommon today in many circles that claim to be based on the pillars of the Reformation. Even now, many explain Peter's quote figuratively and spiritually and say that this is meant for the elect children among them.

But our forefathers taught that we should not interpret this text that way. Calvin says in his commentary regarding Acts 2:39:

> This place therefore does abundantly refute the manifest error of the Anabaptists, which will not have infants, which are the children of the faithful, to be baptized, as if they were not members of the Church. They espy a starting hole in the allegorical sense, and they expound it thus, that by children are meant those which are spiritually begotten. But this gross impudence does nothing to help them. It is plain and evident that Peter spoke thus because God did adopt one nation peculiarly. And circumcision did declare that the right of adoption was common even unto infants. Therefore, even as God made His covenant with Isaac, being as yet unborn, because he was the seed of Abraham, so Peter teaches, that all the children of the Jews are contained in the same covenant, because this promise is always in force, I will be the God of your seed.

Of course, in practice, there are two kinds of seed of Abraham: a seed after the flesh and a spiritual seed. However, this does not annul the fact that they all were comprehended in the covenant. The promises and privileges of the covenant were also for the children of the Israelites.

We see again and again in the Scriptures that the covenant and its external privileges do not apply only to adults, but also to the children. For example, the Lord says in Deuteronomy

1:39, "Moreover your little ones, which ye said should be a prey, and your children, which in that day had no knowledge between good and evil, they shall go in thither, and unto them will I give it, and they shall possess it." Furthermore, the children also shared in the deliverance from bondage in Egypt. The Lord says to Israel, "Let your little ones also go with you." Clearly the children were delivered from Egypt as a fruit of the covenant God made with their fathers. The baptism form therefore defends infant baptism against the Anabaptists, and points out the great privileges of the children of Christians.

"But," you will say, "Peter only talks about the children of the Jews, and not of the children of the Gentiles." Then continue reading what Peter further says, "And to all that are afar off, even as many as the Lord our God shall call." "Afar off" means the Gentiles. The apostle Paul says to the Ephesians, who by nature were Gentiles, "But now in Christ Jesus ye who sometimes were far off are made nigh by the blood of Christ" (2:13). These Gentiles are said to be "afar off"—a proper biblical expression for the misery of the Gentiles. They were far from the salvation of God's covenant, far from the message of salvation, far from the Word of God, and far from the knowledge of the only true God and the Messiah, Jesus Christ.

Peter, however, sees the covenant of God approaching those who are yet afar off. With the coming of Christ, God's covenant is revealed in a different form. The middle wall of partition between Jew and Gentiles has been broken down by Christ, and the blessings of Abraham have come to the Gentiles also. Under the New Testament, the gospel is extended unto those that are "afar off." The covenant of God is revealed more fully. In essence it remains the same covenant, but it is revealed and administered differently. The promise made unto Abraham is now also for the Gentiles. The Apostle Paul says in Galatians 3:14, "That the blessing of Abraham might come on the Gentiles through Jesus Christ."

But there is a restriction: "Even as many as the Lord our God shall call." Peter wants to clarify that not all will share in this privilege. Not everyone will be reached with the message of the gospel. In the Old Testament the promises were only for the Jews; the Gentiles were considered dogs. The Lord Jesus said to the Canaanite woman, "It is not meet to take the children's bread, and to cast it to dogs" (Matt. 15:26). Under the New Testament, however, the middle wall of partition between Jew and Gentile has been broken down. And yet a sovereign restriction remains. According to His sovereign good pleasure, the Lord does not send the gospel to all. Writing about the words of Acts 2:39, "and to all that are afar off, even as many as the LORD our God shall call," Calvin says,

> The Gentiles are named in the last place, which were before strangers. For those which refer it unto the Jews who were exiled afar off (and driven) into far countries, they are greatly deceived. For he speaks not in this place of the distance of place; for he notes a difference between the Jews and the Gentiles, that they were first joined to God by reason of the covenant, and so, consequently, became of his family or household; but the Gentiles were banished from his Kingdom. Paul uses the same speech in the second chapter to the Ephesians (Eph. 2:12) that the Gentiles, which were strangers from the promises, are now drawn near, through Jesus Christ, unto God. Because that Christ (the wall of separation being taken away) has reconciled both (the Jews and Gentiles) unto the Father, and coming, he has preached peace unto those which were nigh at hand, and which were afar off. Now we understand Peter's meaning. For to the end he may amplify the grace of Christ, he does so offer the same unto the Jews, that he said the Gentiles are also partakers thereof. And therefore he uses this word call, as if he should say: Like as God has gathered you together into one peculiar people heretofore by his voice, so the same voice shall sound everywhere, that those which are afar off may come and join themselves unto you, when they shall be called by a new proclamation.

Calvin saw in Peter's words the extension of the administration of God's covenant. It would now be administered to the Gentiles as it was administered to the Jews under the Old Testament. However, a restriction still remains: "even as many as the Lord our God shall call." The voice of the gospel will be heard everywhere—not only in Israel, but among the Gentiles also. God sovereignly determines who will hear the voice of the gospel; even the external call is not for all. It will come only to those to whom God in His good pleasure sends His gospel. Even though the gospel went out to the Gentiles on the day of Pentecost, it did not go to all. Some have not yet heard the Word of God. Think of the many Gentiles who have never heard of God and Christ, who still sit in darkness under shadow of death. They have no means of salvation and Satan still rules undisturbed. Think of those millions of people caught in the lie of Buddhism or Islam. Only a third of mankind belongs externally to Christianity, including the Roman Catholic Church. We realize all the more how privileged we are to live under a pure administration of the gospel. Let us be conscious of our privilege, so that we do not become like Esau, who despised his birthright and afterwards "found no place of repentance, though he sought it carefully with tears" (Heb. 12:17). To be born within the bonds of God's covenant and then go lost will mean to be cast out as a child of the kingdom.

"And to all that are afar off, even as many as the Lord our God shall call." With these words, God's covenant is carried over the borders of the Old Testament into the New Testament. Peter had the Gentiles in mind.

We may take this further and say, as the form said before, "and therefore unto us and our children." To all who are born under the administration of the gospel, the divine word is, "The promise is unto you and to your children." This must be understood to be an earnest and genuine offer of God's grace to those who are born under God's covenant. They are given access to the covenant promises and the door to the benefits of salvation is opened to them. Jacobus Fruytier says, "Those who are baptized may conclude from this: I am not excluded from the kingdom of God and from the eternal covenant, but this is graciously and earnestly offered to me by such a God, who is so gracious as He shows Himself to be in this covenant, and who has prepared such a kingdom for His people" (*The Great Privilege of Children of Christians*, p. 145).

These last words, "as many as the Lord our God shall call," are sometimes seen as a restriction by God concerning the inward calling. The external call of the gospel will go to the Gentiles, but even then, not to all Gentile nations. The Lord will send His gospel "to whom He will and at what time He pleaseth" (Canons of Dort, Head I, Article 3).

"The promise is unto you." This was what Peter said to the mixed multitude because of their external relationship with Abraham and the covenant of grace, and now God says the same to all who belong to the visible church. It is an earnest and genuine offer of God's promises.

Peter told the Jews that they took precedence over the Gentiles. Christ is first the Savior of the Jews and then of the Gentiles. God calls to those who through baptism are in an external relationship with His covenant, "The promise is unto you." Therefore, those who say that baptism promises nothing to the children of the church do not agree with the form for the administration of baptism. Calvin was opposed to interpreting "your children" to be the elect and spiritual children of Abraham. He strongly argues against the Anabaptists and says at the end of his argument, "But if they mean, as they not obscurely show, that the spiritual promise was never made to the carnal seed of Abraham, they are greatly mistaken" (*Institutes*, 4.16.12). Calvin's viewpoint is clear, and yet there have been many arguments about the promises. Therefore, we will consider these things in greater depth.

The Covenant Promises

Thomas Boston says of the covenant of grace, "The covenant is described to us, by the Holy Ghost, as a cluster of free promises of grace and glory to poor sinners, in which no mention is made of any condition" (*Complete Works*, 8:460). The covenant of grace is a covenant of promises. It consists of the promise of salvation and of peace with God. However, when we read these promises in the Bible, we often find that they are conditional. Why can Boston say, "In which no mention is made of any condition?" For example, we read in Isaiah 59:20, "And the Redeemer shall come to Zion, and unto them that turn from transgression in Jacob, saith the LORD." How then can we speak of unconditional promises? The answer must be that the conditional part in the covenant is also a *promise*. How should we understand this?

Well, the things that the Lord requires, such as repentance, faith, coming unto Him, walking in His statutes, etc., are the very things promised in the covenant of grace. The Lord promises to give a new heart, to work faith, to make us walk in His statutes, and to grant perseverance to the end. We can read this clearly in Ezekiel 36 and Jeremiah 31. So, even though we could speak of conditions, the covenant in essence is solely a covenant of promise. Everything is promised to God's elect. The conditions in the promise point out *the way* in which the promises are received. But, in essence, God's covenant is entirely one-sided.

All the conditions of the covenant have been fulfilled by Christ and all requirements to become a partaker of the covenant have been merited by Him. The conditions of the promises are not to be fulfilled in man's own strength, but are a work of God *in* man, or, according to the Canons of Dort, "which God works in us without our aid" (Head III-IV, Article 12). The conditions mentioned with the promises show how we partake of the essence of the promise. It does not mean that we ourselves must take care of the fulfillment of these promises.

The question now is, "To whom are the promises made?" If we listen to Peter, we can answer, "To the church and her seed." He says, "For the promise is unto you." But when we read that the promises are made to everyone who is baptized, a problem arises: how can this be, when we consider what happens in reality? Many who are baptized harden themselves; how can the promise be to them? It seems as if the promising God does not have the strength to fulfill His promises.

The Reformers also struggled with this apparent disparity between God's promise and reality. They usually answered that, in baptism, the promises are sealed and offered to all, but that they are applied to the elect only. In the elect, God works what He requires: repentance and faith. Baptism is compared to preaching of the gospel. That the invitation of the gospel bears fruit with some but not with others does not point to a flaw in the invitation, but points to the work of the Holy Spirit. Through the applying work of the Spirit, God works repentance and faith. Similarly, the covenant promises are sealed and offered unto all who are baptized, but God fulfills the promise in His elect. He remains the free and sovereign Lord.

Therefore, what Calvin emphasizes—that baptism's promises are made to us and to our children—still stands. Calvin was convinced that the promises are for us and our children. According to God's sovereignty, the promises are fulfilled in the elect of the seed of the church.

Calvin goes so far as to say that even when a baptized person rejects God's promise, God's promise still stands. The gospel remains the gospel and Christ remains Christ, even though many reject both. Likewise, the sacrament remains a seal of God's covenant and promise, even though many despise both their baptism and God's promise in it. Calvin comes to this conclusion when he says, "It is irrational to contend that sacraments are not manifestations of divine grace toward us, because they are held forth to the ungodly also, who, however, so far from experiencing God to be more propitious to them, only incur greater condemnation. By the same reasoning, the gospel will be no manifestation of the grace of God, because it is spurned by many who hear it; nor will Christ himself be a manifestation of grace, because of many by whom he was seen and known, very few received him" (*Institutes*, 4.14.7). It is not a matter of a rational scheme. But God is in earnest when He seals His promises in baptism unto us and unto our children. It is because of our unbelief and hardness of heart that the promises are to us of no effect. So we read in Hebrews 4:1: "For unto us was the gospel preached, as well as unto them; but the word preached did not profit them, not being mixed with faith in them that heard it."

Therefore, the promises are offered to all, but, according to God's sovereignty, they are *applied* to the elect. Note, however, that hidden election may not be our starting point. The Canons of Dort say, "As many as are called by the gospel, are unfeignedly called. For God has most earnestly and truly declared in his Word, what will be acceptable to him; namely that all who are called, should comply with this invitation. He, moreover, seriously promises eternal life, and rest, to as many as shall come to him, and believe on him" (Head III-IV, Article 8). The divine invitation is unfeigned and earnest, accompanied by the tears of Jesus shed over a rejecting Jerusalem. Paul says, "As though God did beseech you by us: we pray you in Christ's stead, be ye reconciled to God" (2 Cor. 5:20).

Though many go lost under this invitation, this is not God's fault, but that of man who has hardened himself. Nevertheless, the purpose of God will be fulfilled. He will work in the elect what He requires: repentance towards God and faith in Christ Jesus. The rejection of many will not destroy the salvation of God's elect and the fulfillment of His promises. In the offer of the gospel, the promises are held out to all who hear it. The message is, "For the promise is unto you and your children."

Concerning the promises of the covenant, Boston says,

Christ's promises in his testament are to mankind-sinners, as the promise to Canaan was to the Israelites in Egypt, indefinitely, those not excepted whose carcasses fell in the wilderness, Ex. vi.6, "Say unto the children of Israel, I am the Lord." ver. 8, "And I will bring you in unto the land concerning the which I did swear." Thus was there a promise left them of entering into the rest of Canaan: and those who believed it, got the possession accordingly; those who believed not, did lose it. And they fell short of it, not because it was not left to them; but because, though it was left to them, as well as to those that entered, yet they believed it not. So says the apostle, "They could not enter in because of unbelief,"

Heb. iii. 19. And this was no imputation on the faithfulness of God: for even in promises, as well as in covenants, there is a necessity of a mutual consent unto the same thing; the party to whom the promise is made, his acceptance thereof being necessary to complete the obligation on the promiser to make it effectual (*Complete Works*, 8:542-543).

I hope that we can follow Boston's reasoning because it is of utmost importance, if we are to understand the form for the administration of baptism. God's promises were offered to all Israel. Boston says that those who fell in the wilderness had not been excluded from God's promise concerning Canaan; rather, they did not enter because of their unbelief. God's promises are fulfilled in the way of repentance and faith in Jesus Christ.

We are again confronted with what we have discussed before—that a "consenting" or an "assenting" is necessary to truly share in the promises. That they could not enter in, and that many of those who are baptized have not obtained the fulfillment of those promises, is not because of a lack of sincerity of God, but because of the hardened sinner, who loves the world and will fall through unbelief.

This should sufficiently demonstrate that, although the promises are applied to the elect only, they are nevertheless offered to all in the administration of the covenant. In baptism, God seals the truth of His promises and His invitation.

These two aspects of baptism are found in the views of Scottish theologians Ebenezer and Ralph Erskine and James Fisher. In their booklet, "The Covenant of Grace," which Rev. Kersten attempted to publish just before his death, they interpreted the words, "For the promise is unto you," to mean a dual right to the promise. They distinguished between a right of access and a right of possession. They showed that God's election is glorified in the covenant of grace because the essence of the covenant concerns God's elect, while in the administration of the covenant the promises come to all who hear the gospel. The all-sufficiency of the Mediator of the covenant and the free promises of God allow for an unrestricted administration of the covenant of grace, and the gospel must therefore be offered to all.

Q. 82: To whom are the covenant promises presented?
A.: To those who hear the gospel with their seed. Acts 2:39, "For the promise is unto you, and to your children."

Q. 83: What right to the promises have they who hear the gospel when these are presented unto them without distinction?
A.: A right to accept the promises and all the benefits contained therein, so that they are not to be excused when they do not believe them.

Q. 84: What right to the promises does faith or the deed of believing give?
A.: A right of possession, which is based on the union with Christ in whom all the promises are Yea and Amen. John 3:36, "He that believeth on the Son hath everlasting life."

These questions and answers show that everyone who is baptized and all hearers of the gospel have a right of access and a right to use the promises. Only faith gives a right of possession. Only by repentance and faith can we come to possess what has been promised.

It is important to distinguish between these rights. We have to be aware of two dangers: first, there is the danger of minimizing the genuine offer of God in the gospel; secondly, there is a danger that we simply apply the promises to ourselves without repentance and faith. Baptism says to those who are baptized, "The promise is unto you." Many say, "I accept the promises and apply them to myself to be my personal possession, and therefore I am saved." But by applying the promises to ourselves without faith in Christ, we deceive ourselves. À Brakel speaks so often of the evangelical offer and of coming to God on the basis of His promises, and says that there are no promises in the Bible at all for these people. He says, "It will be beneficial to answer the following question: Is it not possible to apply a promise wrongly to one's self? Answer: There are no promises for the unconverted in the Bible. They deceive themselves, regardless of what promises they appropriate to themselves" (*The Christian's Reasonable Service*, 2:632).

We need to pay attention here. À Brakel speaks about the *appropriation* of the promises. He deals with the life of faith on the promises, which concerns the trusting in faith upon the promises of God, and warns that an unconverted person may not simply appropriate the promise to himself and say, "Now I will be saved, because God has promised it." Whoever does this appropriates the promise wrongly and deceives himself. À Brakel also says, "When considering a promise, one must carefully note to whom the promise is made. To appropriate promises to oneself without having a foundation for doing so is great foolishness and imagination; this will deceive the soul unto her destruction" (*The Christian's Reasonable Service*, 2:618). A vain boasting in the covenant promises without conversion to God and faith in Christ Jesus will bring us to destruction.

To those who bear the sign of baptism as a seal of their incorporation in the Christian church, God says, "For the promise is unto you, and to your children." There is, however, a right of access, which is to come pleading on the promises, and a right of possession. À Brakel says, "The entire efficacy of baptism consists in this—that it seals the covenant of grace and all its promises to the child. This is not to suggest that the child has them already, but rather that the child is entitled to them." This is what is meant by the words "The promise is unto you." Use them in a holy manner and take it to the Lord saying, "Do as Thou hast said."

I know that many abuse this. That is why I have paid so much attention to the true meaning of Peter's words. Paul's words will apply to them: "Behold, ye despisers, and wonder, and perish" (Acts 13:41).

To those who stagger at the promise and focus on their own unworthiness, I say, "Remember that Christ is the door to the promise." Promises are made to sinners as sinners, not to righteous ones.

Circumcision

The form continues its defense of infant baptism and says: "Therefore God formerly commanded them to be circumcised, which was a seal of the covenant, and of the righteousness of faith." This statement reiterates what has been said before, proving that children are also comprehended in God's covenant.

This proof starts with the word "Therefore." Because the promise was not only to the adults but also to the children, God wanted to seal His covenant with Israel in their children; He therefore commanded them to be circumcised. The promises of the covenant were the reason for the children's circumcision. The children were part of the church of Israel, as we read very clearly in Joel 2:16: "Gather the people, sanctify the congregation, assemble the elders, gather the children, and those that suck the breasts." Furthermore, the Lord expressly says that the children of the Israelites were His possession. It is striking to read this in Ezekiel 16:21, when the Lord condemns an idolatrous Israel: "Thou hast slain my children, and delivered them to cause them to pass through the fire for them." The children sacrificed by the Israelites to the abominable service of Moloch were *God's* children. The Lord says to their parents, "What did you do to My children?" Parents, take heed to what the Lord says here. In the covenant relationship, they are His children. One day we will stand before God's judgment seat and be asked by the Lord, "What did you do to My children?" Our children belong to God and His service. How terrible to have sacrificed them to this world!

The children were comprehended in the covenant of God and thus they received the seal of that covenant, which was circumcision. The same must be said of our children. Because they are born to Christian parents, they are comprehended in God's covenant and therefore they must be baptized.

The Anabaptists reject this and say that circumcision belonged to a time period when the church was in its infancy. They say that under the new covenant, the church has the Spirit, and therefore such signs are no longer necessary. However, such excuses do not hold when the Scriptures clearly speak about circumcision as being a sign and seal of God's covenant. The Reformer Henry Bullinger particularly defended this principle of the Reformation against the Anabaptists. He writes, "Perhaps someone would say that the little children of Christians do not believe. I accept this, but the children of Jews did not believe either, and yet they were circumcised and were comprehended in the covenant of God" (*Sermons*, 172-173; Ursprung, 114-116).

Bullinger admits that the children who are baptized cannot yet exercise faith. However, this is no hindrance for them to be baptized, as the children of the Jews were circumcised when they could not exercise faith either. Our children are baptized on the same basis—namely, because of God's covenant and promises.

Circumcision was essentially a minor operation; a mark was cut into the flesh of the Israelite children. Thus Israel was a marked nation, a people owned by God. Likewise, baptism marks us. The saying is true that the flames of hell can never wipe away the water of baptism. The children of the visible church bear God's mark on their foreheads. It says what circumcision said of Israel: "These people are separate." The Lord says, "From all the nations of the earth you only have I known." This brings with it the duty to be dedicated to Him and to be separated from the world to fear and to serve God. You carry a mark, children and young people! Take heed so that this sign brings you profit and blessing; if you do not, it will forever burn on your soul that you carried this mark but disregarded it.

Through circumcision, the Israelite children came into a special relationship with God. God set them apart. This applies also to all who are baptized, both adults and children. We ought to be separate and to bring forth fruits worthy of faith and repentance.

The form says more about circumcision: "which was a seal of the covenant, and of the righteousness of faith." We have discussed how circumcision is a seal and mark. Now we will consider what "the righteousness of faith" means.

The phrase is taken from Romans 4:11, where the apostle

Paul says, "And he [Abraham] received the sign of circumcision, a seal of the righteousness of the faith." Paul argues in Romans 4 that Abraham was not justified through the works of the law, but through faith in Christ. Based on his faith in Christ, he received circumcision as a seal that he was truly justified before God. The Dutch annotations on Romans 4:11 say, "These words summarize the nature and properties of all sacraments (signs of the covenant) as in Genesis 17:11, Exodus 12:13, and Ezekiel 20:12. They serve not first to work faith, but to seal and to strengthen it. And therefore, they are not mere signs, but also seals."

Paul argues that Abraham believed in Christ even before he was circumcised and therefore that he was justified before God; after that, he received circumcision as a seal of the justification through faith. Thus, circumcision sealed to him that he was justified before God in Christ. It sealed God's grace to his heart; God fixed His seal to His covenant and promises. Viewed from God's side, this was unnecessary, since He is the Truth Himself. But the Lord did this for Abraham's sake—to strengthen his faith.

The circumcised and baptized children are seals that confirm the truth of God's covenant and promises. The Lord confirms in the baptism of children what is sung after the administration of baptism, "Jehovah's truth will stand forever, His covenant-bonds He will not sever" (Psalter 425, verse 5).

For Abraham and the Old Testament believers, circumcision was a seal of the truth and certainty of God's promises. Baptism now has the same efficacy. The baptized person does not need to doubt whether God is sincere when He says to him, "For the promise is unto you." His baptized forehead is a seal of it. Furthermore, true believers receive the same confirmation Abraham received: they are justified before God.

Christ Embracing the Children
And therefore Christ also embraced them, laid his hands upon them and blessed them.

As a further proof for infant baptism, the authors now point to what Christ did. Under the Old Testament, the children were comprehended in the covenant because they received the sacrament of the covenant in circumcision. God's love in the Old Testament was not only manifested to adults, but also to children. The children shared in the sacrament of the covenant.

According to human reasoning, God's command to Abraham should have been, "Circumcise yourself and those in your household who are capable of understanding this symbol." However, according to the law of divine love, the command was, "And he that is eight days old shall be circumcised among you, every man child in your generations... and my covenant shall be in your flesh for an everlasting covenant" (Gen. 17:12-13). This divine love has not diminished under the New Testament. The Lord Jesus approved and confirmed the institution of His Father to also include children in the covenant by embracing them and laying His hands on them. He did not exclude children from God's kingdom. He crowned marriage by honoring it through His presence, His gifts, and His miracles at Cana in Galilee. And He evidenced God's love toward Israel's seed by receiving and embracing their children.

Calvin, who excelled others in understanding the deeds of Christ, said, "Hence our Lord Jesus Christ, to give an example from which the world might learn that he had come to enlarge rather than to limit the grace of the Father, kindly takes the little children in his arms, and rebukes his disciples for attempting to prevent them from coming" (*Institutes*, 4.16.7).

Christ's task was to seek and to save that which was lost— not only adults, but children also. His embrace of the children clearly shows us God's mercy toward them. The word "brought" in Mark 10 ("And they brought young children to him"), can also be translated as "carried," showing that the children were very young or newborn infants. Christ said, "Suffer the little children to come unto me, and forbid them not: for of such is the kingdom of God" (Mark 10:14).

The Anabaptists, sensing how much this deed of Jesus condemns their view of excluding the children from the sacrament of baptism, have tried to remove the meaning from these words of Jesus. They have given a different meaning to the word "such." They say that Jesus meant that we can only inherit the kingdom of God when we are as helpless and dependent as a child. And indeed, the Lord Jesus once taught this by placing a child in the middle of the disciples and saying, "Verily I say unto you, Except ye be converted, and become as little children, ye shall not enter into the kingdom of heaven" (Matt. 18:3). However, that was a different occasion and does not have the same meaning as here.

The Dutch annotations explain what the Lord Jesus had in mind: "These are the children of the covenant, as were the children of the Jews. Otherwise, the children of unbelievers are called unclean, 1 Corinthians 7:14." This concerns the covenant relationship. The Lord Jesus said the same thing as Peter, "For the promise is unto you, and to your children"—just in different words. Thus, circumcision shows that the covenant of God includes children, as does the Lord Jesus' embracing of children.

Fruytier explains Jesus embracing the children as follows:

> Who can refuse the water to those, whom Jesus invites unto Himself, whom He embraces with His arms, who may be cleansed through His blood and Spirit, unto whom is the promise of the covenant of grace and whom God expressly allows to be called holy? It is evident that the infants spoken of were carried by others. It is for this reason that the disciples resented this as they judged such ones unfit to be instructed by Jesus. Jesus, who wanted to show that such children were to be admitted to outwardly enjoy His favor, grace and love, forbids His disciples to rebuke those who were bringing such children unto Him, thereby showing that one has to help and encourage those who bring the children. He also shows that such children have need of His grace, for of such is the kingdom of heaven, that is, the kingdom of both grace and glory. When Jesus now deals and speaks in this manner it is as if He says, "If there be parents or friends, whose desire it is to bring

their children unto Me, then hinder them not, but encourage them just as I have done by putting My hands upon them as a sign of the blessing which I give unto them" (*The Great Privilege of Children of Christians,* 124-125).

Parents, if only we all, realizing the misery of our children, were driven to bring them to Jesus. Surely He would not cast us out; Christ would do as He said, "Suffer little children, and forbid them not, to come unto me: for of such is the kingdom of heaven."

Children, the Lord Jesus has said that He is willing to receive you. He says, "Suffer little children to come unto me," even when you do many things wrong, even when you are very sinful.

I hope that this will spur both parents and children to flee to Christ. God described this event in His Word for that very reason. May the Lord grant that we baptize our children in the same spirit as those mothers who carried their children to Jesus. Fruytier says, "Did not Jesus take the children who were brought unto Him into His arms and bless them? In baptism He does likewise, promising them that if they are raised for Him and if they do not despise the blood through which they are sanctified (Heb. 10:29) and made nigh (Eph. 2:13), He shall wash them in His blood and Spirit and they will be accepted by the Father as His children" (ibid., p. 103).

Christ is now in heaven, but He has not changed. Therefore, parents need not doubt that Christ loves to receive children still today, as Jesus Christ is the same yesterday, and today, and forever.

Heirs of the Covenant
Since then baptism is come in the place of circumcision, therefore infants are to be baptized as heirs of the kingdom of God, and of his covenant.

Baptism has come in the place of circumcision, and it is important for the church to understand this. In the early Christian church, both sacraments existed together for some time. The Lord Jesus received both sacraments, uniting in Himself both

the Old Testament and the New Testament. Yet the New Testament church had to relinquish the bloody circumcision and
administer the bloodless sign of baptism. We read in Paul's letters how he had to battle against the desire of the Jewish
Christians to hold fast to circumcision.

However, God's providence with His church has been such
that the authors of the form can say: "Since then baptism is
come in the place of circumcision...." With the shedding of
Christ's blood, all the ceremonial shedding of blood ended,
including the shedding of blood in circumcision. There was no
need for it anymore; in fact, it was no longer allowed. All shad-
ows were fulfilled in Christ; a better covenant was revealed, and
this therefore required a new sacrament. Now females would
also receive the sign of the covenant and become full members
of the Christian church.

Paul writes to the uncircumcised Christians at Colosse, "In
whom also ye are circumcised...by the circumcision of Christ:
buried with him in baptism" (Col. 2:11-12). Notice that he calls
baptism the circumcision of Christ. What does this mean? It
means nothing less than that baptism has come in the place of
circumcision. We must realize that all blessings, privileges,
promises, and obligations have passed from circumcision to
baptism. The privileges of the circumcised Jews now also apply
to the baptized Gentiles. Those privileges of the Jews are mentioned in Romans 9:4, where we read, "Who are Israelites; to
whom pertaineth the adoption, and the glory, and the
covenants, and the giving of the law, and the service of God,
and the promises."

Having come in the place of circumcision, baptism means
that the blessings promised to Abraham are now for the Gentiles. The church now shares in the great privilege that was first
given to the Jews. Fruytier says, "This again is no small privilege as when, according to God's command, the children are
baptized, they receive the covenant of God in their flesh, as
the circumcised children of Abraham (Gen. 17:13). Through
baptism the children are separated from the ungodly world

and they are dedicated to God. They receive the seal that they were born to be God's" (*The Great Privilege of Children of Christians*, p. 103).

The Belgic Confession of Faith says in Article 34, "And that He, having abolished circumcision, which was done with blood, has instituted the sacrament of baptism instead thereof; by which we are received into the Church of God, and separated from all other people and strange religions, that we may wholly belong to him, whose ensign and banner we bear; and which serves as a testimony to us, that he will forever be our gracious God and Father." We trust that these words sufficiently explained the first few words of this part of the form.

"Therefore, infants are to be baptized as heirs of the kingdom of God, and of his covenant." Earlier in the form, the children were called "children of wrath." Now they are called heirs of the kingdom of God and of His covenant. Of course, we must realize that the form has not forgotten the former title; the author's intention is to point out why the children of the visible church are to be baptized. "Therefore children are to be baptized." Why? Because they are heirs of the kingdom of God and of His covenant.

Why were the children of the Israelites circumcised, whereas the children of the Gentiles were not? Why may a child of Christian parents be baptized, but a child of heathen and unbaptized parents may not? Only because the children of the Israelites belonged to a people whom God had separated and chosen for Himself, and so it is with baptism. The children who belong to the visible church are to be baptized. The children of the Israelites did not become Israelites through their circumcision; rather, they were circumcised because they were Israelites. The same applies to baptism. The children are privileged children as they are born within the boundaries of the covenant and therefore are to be baptized.

We may illustrate this with a child who is born to American parents on American soil. Because of his birth, the child is an American citizen. His entry in the registry of births proves it.

The child does not become an American citizen when he is registered, but is registered because he is an American.

Perhaps it sounds a bit strange to us when we read that the children of the visible church are called heirs of the kingdom of God and of His covenant. This wording could make us think of the elect and of the partakers of Christ's benefits. However, this is not the intention. If we do not understand this wording correctly, it is because we are not acquainted with the language of the Bible. Remember that the Lord Jesus called the carnal Jews, who rejected Him, "children of the kingdom." The Dutch annotations say, "These are the Jews with whom God had indeed made an external covenant, but who made themselves unworthy thereof through their unbelief." Hence, the Lord Jesus called them children of the covenant because of their relationship to the covenant of God. Likewise, we must understand the authors' language. Because of the children's relationship to God's covenant, they are called heirs of the kingdom of God and of His covenant. We must not interpret this to mean that all children have received saving grace. The apostle Peter addresses the unbelieving Jews also as children of the covenant (Acts 3:25), but he does not stop there. He calls those children of the covenant to repentance and says, "Repent ye therefore and be converted." John the Baptist also said to the circumcised Jews, "Bring forth therefore fruits worthy of repentance." The Lord Jesus did likewise when He pointed out to Abraham's descendants that they should do Abraham's works.

So we should not immediately interpret these words to mean saving grace, but we should see the great privilege our children share because of their being born in the visible church. Bernardus Smytegelt says, "At that place God gathers His church; there the Lord Jesus visits His people and there is the great opportunity for a sinner to be converted to God."

By nature, children born into the visible church are as condemned as any other children, but, through God's favor, they are separated and bear the name of "children of the kingdom" and "children of the covenant." The form has given these meaningful names to our children. We read the name "heir." An heir is someone who will inherit something. The Israelites who descended from Abraham were Abraham's heirs; they inherited their great privilege from Abraham. The children of the visible church are, through their birth, heirs as well; they inherit their great privilege because of their birth from Christian parents. On the one hand, our children are heirs of Adam, but, on the other hand, they are born among people to whom God has given His promises. Heirs of God are not found among the fallen angels or among those who never have heard of God or Christ. They are found where His Word is preached: in the heart of the church. There, Jesus is offering peace and pardon and the Holy Spirit brings sinners to conversion.

It is a great privilege to live where God's Word is preached and where we can hear the footsteps of those who proclaim the good tidings of the gospel. God gave you the privilege of being born where His Word is preached. That is why Jesus calls us "children of the kingdom" and the form calls us "heirs of the kingdom of God and of His covenant."

But note well that someone can be called a child of the kingdom and yet be cast out. We can be called branches of the vine and yet be burned with everlasting fire. We can be called an heir and yet through unbelief never become a possessor of the offered inheritance. We should not forget this! We must not think we are saved just because we carry the covenant externally; we would be mistaken eternally. In accordance with the words of Jesus, we must do the works of Abraham. Because of our privilege, we may carry beautiful names—"children of the kingdom," "branches," "children of the covenant and of the prophets"—and yet miss out on the eternal inheritance through unbelief and hardening our hearts.

The Bible and the men of the Reformation make the same point. Thomas Boston speaks clearly about the legacy of the covenant when he says, "Our Lord Jesus has made such a testament: the lost family of Adam, is the family constituted his legatees: and the gospel is the lawful intimation made to them, to

come to the executor and receive their legacies. All that believe
get the legacy; all unbelievers lose it, and perish under the want
thereof; and they perish without excuse. They cannot pretend
that there was nothing left them by the testator; which is the case
of the fallen angels: nor yet, that it was not intimated unto them;
which is the case of those that never heard the gospel. But they
perish, because, howbeit there was a rich legacy left them, yet
they undervalued the testator's kindness, and would never come
and claim it by faith" (*Complete Works*, 8:542).

How terrible to have known of the testament through the
preaching of the gospel; not to have belonged to the excluded
devils, but to have heard that the benefits of the testament are
intended for the sinners of Adam's family; and yet to be cast out
eternally. It would be better to have never been born. How deep
and serious are the words of Jesus: "But the children of the
kingdom shall be cast out into outer darkness."

Fruytier, speaking about the privilege of hearing the gospel,
says, "A believing parent, considering all this, may say: Now my
children are not excluded from the kingdom of God, but they
are invited by Christ who said: Suffer the little children to come
unto me, and forbid them not: for of such is the kingdom of
God. The bread of the children also is for them, as they are no
longer considered dogs by Jesus" (*The Great Privilege of Children
of Christians*, p. 103).

The form calls the children of the visible church heirs of the
kingdom of God and of His covenant. This does not contradict
God's eternal plan. At the end of time, Romans 11:7 will apply
to the visible church of the Gentiles as well as it was applied to
the Old Testament church of the Jews: "What then? Israel hath
not obtained that which he seeketh for; but the election hath
obtained it, and the rest were blinded." This will be the final outcome. Even though the inheritance is despised and scorned by
many—even by those whom Jesus called the children of the
kingdom—yet the counsel of God shall come to pass. Calvin
says in his commentary on Titus 3:5, "Although by baptism
wicked men are neither washed nor renewed, yet it retains that

power, so far as relates to God, because, although they reject the grace of God, still it is offered to them." They will never be able to deny that grace was offered to them.

The form says that children are to be baptized. There is no express command in the Bible to baptize children; we believe that such a command was not necessary. Calvin says that the children are comprehended in Christ's command to baptize all nations. To the administration of the covenant of grace belongs the preaching of the gospel as well as the administration of the sacraments. Therefore, Jesus did not only give a command to preach, but also to baptize (Matt. 28:19).

We know that complete households were baptized. The Bible tells us of Lydia and her household (Acts 16:15), of the jailer and all his household (Acts 16:33), and of the household of Stephanas (1 Cor. 1:16). Further, there are testimonies from the early Christian church that speak of infant baptism. Cyprian, who died in the year 258, was asked whether it was necessary to postpone infant baptism until the eighth day; he replied that this was not necessary. The church father Origen, who died in the year 254, said, "According to the custom of the church, baptism is administered unto children also. The church received this custom—to baptize the children—from the apostles." Augustine said, "The entire church agrees that children are to be baptized. This has not been instituted by a synod, but has been done by apostolic authority and the custom has been practiced since."

We must consider the accounts of baptizing households as proof that a family or household is seen as a whole integral unit. Herein we see the line of the covenant of grace: "For the promise is unto you, and to your children." God includes the children of believers in His covenant.

It was not without reason that we quoted early church fathers. It is especially important to be aware of what the early Christian church said, as there are many groups who say that the early Christian church did not practice infant baptism. But in the early Christian church the children were baptized, and, according to Augustine, by "apostolic authority."

Calvin's form for the administration of baptism describes the need to baptize children as follows: "Although the children are from the depraved race of Adam, yet He accepts them through the power of this covenant with Abraham and his seed, to count them among the number of His children. Therefore, it was His will from the beginning that the children in His church would receive the sign of circumcision, whereby He then presented what is now shown unto us by baptism."

The Duty of the Parents

And parents are in duty bound, further to instruct their children herein, when they shall arrive to years of discretion.

The form now discusses the duty of the parents. The defense of infant baptism began with stating that the child was not aware of his fall in Adam or of the deliverance through Christ. The form said, "And although our young children do not understand these things...." So the child is still unaware of these things. However, he will grow up and begin to reason, and then the parents have the duty to instruct the child further. Children must be taught what God's covenant means as they grow up. Through repentance and faith, they must become true partakers of the covenant blessings and bring forth fruits of repentance and faith. If they do not, they will be cast out of the kingdom. They will not enter into God's rest because of unbelief.

A great responsibility rests upon the baptized child. Yet this responsibility does not only rest on the children, but also on parents. They should be like priests, pleading on the promises of God on behalf of their children and wrestling with God in prayer for their conversion. They should be as prophets, teaching their children about the demands and promises of God's covenant. They should be as kings, demanding obedience to God from their children and acknowledgment of Him as their Lord.

Parents teach children. They teach them to walk, talk, read, count, obey, and become independent. But the parents are also called to teach their children about God and His service. They must bring them up in the fear of God. Children must hear from their parents about God as the Creator of all things, about the fall in paradise, about Christ who came into this world to save sinners, about the necessity of conversion and faith in Christ Jesus, and about what baptism means.

Children are largely dependent on those who raise them. In the first few years of life, the child receives impressions that remain throughout his entire life. Many things in life can be traced back to our first few years of life. Nine out of ten people have become what they are now through the way their parents raised them. Children follow in the footsteps of their parents.

What a great responsibility parents have for their children! When children are young, you should think, "Now is our time to sow." What is sown in the younger years can, under God's blessing, be harvested later. We focus so much on materialistic things with our children. Far too often, we raise our children with one goal in mind: they must be successful in this world. But the goal of upbringing in Israel did not focus on performance. The main goal was to learn the fear of the Lord and the knowledge of His deeds. The Lord said of Abraham, "For I know him, that he will command his children and his household after him, and they shall keep the way of the LORD, to do justice and judgment; that the LORD may bring upon Abraham that which he hath spoken of him" (Gen. 18:19). In Israel, mothers took a very important position in the upbringing of the children. The mother's name of many of the kings of Israel is mentioned to teach us that the son is what the mother made of him. Proverbs 6:20 says, "My son, keep thy father's commandment, and forsake not the law of thy mother." The Israelites were to raise their children so that they would become people who feared the Lord and loved Him for the grace He showed to Israel. Instruction particularly involved telling the children about the deeds of God's grace over Israel and God's wrath over Israel's enemies. The fear of the Lord took the foremost place in the instruction of children.

The New Testament also admonishes the parents to bring up their children in the fear of the Lord. What a holy task rests on parents' shoulders! You cannot and may not shift that task either to the school or church. The Lord demands that you, as parents, teach your children about God and His service, about sin and grace, about Adam and Christ, and about the necessity of conversion and faith. Remember, it concerns the souls of your children! Luther said, "All parents should consider their child a precious eternal treasure, which God has commanded to be kept, so that the devil, the world, and the flesh will not devour it."

This instruction in the ways and precepts of God is, in the first place, the task of the parents. Concerning this, the Synod of Dordrecht spoke of "home catechism." The first instruction a child receives comes from his parents. Instruction by school-teachers and officebearers in catechism class comes afterward.

What then should the parents teach? The form says: "to instruct their children herein." This refers to what the form has said previously.

The form gave only a summary of the doctrine of baptism. The authors only touched on the kernel of the matter; parents have to further instruct. They have to enlarge on it. By the word "herein," the authors intended the meaning of baptism. The children must be instructed in what baptism signifies. When children were baptized, they were so little that they did not understand anything of what happened. When they grow up, parents have to tell and instruct them about the meaning of baptism. Parents must say, "When you were very little, something special happened to you—something very solemn and holy. When you did not even realize who you were, you were baptized in the Name of the triune God. You are a child who lives on holy ground. The Lord has sealed His promises to your forehead."

As fits their intellectual ability, children must be instructed about the three parts of the doctrine of baptism: misery, deliverance, and gratitude. Parents may not forget to speak about man's great misery. Teach your children about the misery of Adam's fall and the just wrath of God. But when you do this, make sure that you always set over against it the saving work of God in Christ Jesus. Speak to them about the great privilege which they received through baptism, and direct them to God who stretches out His arms to them, even before they were able to think about their misery, and who said, "As I live, saith the Lord GOD, I have no pleasure in the death of the wicked; but that the wicked turn from his way and live" (Ezek. 33:11).

When they grow up, the children must understand what baptism means. Besides knowing about sin, they must know about the promises that are sealed on their foreheads. The water of baptism seals to us the washing away of sin in Jesus' blood. The parents must impress on their children's heart the obligation to cleave to the God of this baptism, to fear and to love Him. The children must know what they share in Adam: death and destruction. They must know what is to be found in Christ: life and salvation. While they are still little, they must hear of the great wonders of grace worked by the God of Israel, so that in their tender consciences there will be a deep reverence for God. The child must be instructed about the happiness of those who fear the Lord and of the willingness of Christ to receive children.

Parents are often very guilty in these matters. They speak with their children about everything except what concerns God and the welfare of their souls. In many families, not one word is ever said about the eternal concerns of the soul. Spiritually, the family members are strangers to each other. Parents, take care that you are not guilty of the blood of your children when God will call you to give an account of your stewardship. Seek to be convinced of the value of the immortal souls of your children. It is so necessary to further instruct your children; love for the soul is the soul of all true love. The fathers and mothers who are truly convinced of the value of the souls of their children will take this responsibility to heart. They will instruct their children. The weight of the immortal souls of our children must press on us in such a way that we bring them to

Christ, who said, "Suffer little children to come unto me, and forbid them not."

Parents, remember the examples in the Bible when the instruction of the parents was an eternal blessing for the children. Think of Samuel, Solomon, Timothy, and many others. How Solomon praises his mother who instructed him in the fear of the Lord! Follow in the footsteps of Eunice, who instructed her little son Timothy in the Holy Scriptures and told him the great wonders of Israel's God. Instruct your children. Talk with them, pray with them, wrestle for them with God, so that one day you may shout for joy and say, "He hath remembered his covenant for ever" (Ps. 105:8).

CHAPTER 3

The Prayer

Having discussed the doctrinal part of the form for baptism, we now proceed to consider the part about the liturgy. This consists of a prayer, an exhortation to the parents, the baptismal formula, and the prayer of thanksgiving. It is a very simple liturgy and quite different from the extended liturgy of the Roman Catholic Church.

The prayer is preceded by an exhortation. The congregation is called to lift eyes and hearts heavenward and to call upon the God of baptism. The authors say, "That therefore this holy ordinance of God may be administered to his glory, to our comfort, and to the edification of his Church, let us call upon his holy name." Baptism is here called a holy ordinance of God. It is God who instituted the ordinance of baptism. And there are three reasons why this ordinance must be used: for God's honor, to our comfort, and to edify the church.

In the first place, baptism concerns God's honor. We need to be reminded of this again and again. Everything we do, and certainly baptism, must be done to the honor of God.

In the second place, the administration of baptism should be to our comfort. Comfort is something that each member of the fallen race of man needs, but particularly the parents and the congregation who heard the opening words of the form: "That we with our children are conceived and born in sin, and therefore are children of wrath." The parents also need comfort when they consider their child and the sinful, tempting powers of this present evil world. What will befall this child? What will be the outcome of our upbringing? These are questions that trouble many a parental heart while standing at the baptismal font. Such a parental heart requires comfort, and where can that comfort be found except in the covenant God, who shows visibly in baptism the cleansing power of Jesus' blood? Where else can that comfort be found except with God, who seals visibly in baptism His lovingkindness throughout the generations, to them who remember His covenant? There is comfort to be found for sinners convicted of their sin and guilt. They are called to "arise, and be baptized, and wash away thy sins, calling on the name of the Lord" (Acts 22:16). Baptism also brings comfort to God's children who are so often unfaithful to the covenant of God. Truly, the administration of baptism is to our comfort.

Thirdly, the administration of baptism is to the edification of the church. To edify means to lay a foundation, or to build up. The sacrament edifies the church and strengthens faith. Through baptism, God wants to strengthen His people so that they can say with David, "Although my house be not so with God; yet he hath made with me an everlasting covenant, ordered in all things, and sure" (2 Sam. 23:5). The congregation is edified when baptism is administered. God seals before the congregation that He will continue His work and glorify His Name among their seed, from child to child and from generation to generation.

To achieve this three-fold purpose, the church is exhorted to call upon God's holy name thus:

> O Almighty and eternal God, thou, who hast according to thy severe judgment punished the unbelieving and unrepentant world with the flood, and hast according to thy great mercy saved and protected believing Noah and his family; thou, who hast drowned the obstinate Pharaoh and his host in the Red Sea, and hast led thy people Israel through the midst of the Sea upon dry ground, by which baptism was signified—we beseech thee, that thou wilt be pleased of thine infinite mercy, graciously to look upon these children, and incorporate them by thy Holy Spirit, into thy Son Jesus

Christ, that they may be buried with him into his death, and be raised with him in newness of life; that they may daily follow him, joyfully bearing their cross, and cleave unto him in true faith, firm hope, and ardent love; that they may, with a comfortable sense of thy favor, leave this life, which is nothing but a continual death, and at the last day, may appear without terror before the judgment seat of Christ thy Son, through Jesus Christ our Lord, who with thee and the Holy Ghost, one only God, lives and reigns forever. Amen.

Form prayers are not very popular among us. In the past, many have rejected their use, saying that the prayer must well up freely from the heart. Nevertheless, the men of the Reformation deemed form prayers as a necessary part of the administration of the sacraments and for the ordination of officebearers in the church. They did this to promote unity in profession, in order that personal opinions would not take a prominent position. They also did this so that the congregation would hear how the church views the sacrament. The forms are part of the doctrine of the church concerning baptism. The Dutch synods of 1574 and 1618-19 and later have supported what the forms say.

The opening words are: "O Almighty and eternal God...." The church calls on an almighty and eternal God. The name of the Lord is called upon under deep impressions that the Lord is God and that we are but creatures.

Then the deeds of this almighty and eternal God are considered: "Thou, who hast according to thy severe judgment punished the unbelieving and unrepentant world with the flood, and hast according to thy great mercy saved and protected believing Noah and his family...." In its prayer, the church goes back in history. The congregation calls on God, who in His great mercy spared Noah but destroyed the evil and unrepentant first world by the flood. The prayer reminds the congregation of the saving of Noah and his family. We would say, "What does this have to do with holy baptism?" Yet, the authors say in the form, "by which baptism was signified." When they base this on the history of Noah being saved in the ark, our fathers are not allegorizing Scripture, but are basing their words on God's Word. In 1 Peter 3:20-21 we read, "In the days of Noah, while the ark was a preparing, wherein few, that is, eight souls were saved by water. The like figure whereunto even baptism doth also now save us." The comparison is not a product of the authors' own imaginations but is a truly biblical comparison. The water is symbolic of both the saving of Noah and his family, and the saving of the elect through the washing of regeneration. The Dutch annotations say, "Baptism is called thus, because it is a sacrament of us being saved from the universal destruction of worldly people, like the Ark which was a means of the physical saving of Noah and all his from the destruction of the first world." The water made a separation between Noah's family and the evil first world, so baptism is the separating element between the church and the world. Our baptism means that we ought to be separated from this present evil world.

However, there is more than just an outward separation from the world. Noah's salvation was a salvation from the judgment of God. In the baptismal prayer, we plead for the salvation of our children from a wicked world which, like the first world, does not regard God and is under His judgment. Noah and his family were not just separated from the world, but they were saved from the world. When the world sank, they were saved from the judgment. We pray to God for this grace for our children; the outward separation from the world alone is not enough.

Peter says the same. After having pointed out Noah's salvation, Peter says in verse 21, "Not the putting away of the filth of the flesh, but the answer of a good conscience toward God by the resurrection of Jesus Christ." The Dutch annotations say, "That is, the outward baptism, through which the filthiness of our bodies is washed away, and of which many hypocrites and mouth-Christians are partakers, does not save our souls, but the apostle means to say, that which is inward, and which is applied unto our souls through the blood and the Spirit of Christ."

Outward separation may be a great privilege, but it is not

sufficient for salvation. It was no small matter to be saved in the ark from the destruction of the first world. Likewise, it is a great privilege and an undeserved mercy of God to be separated from the world and to be incorporated into the Christian church through baptism. This brings us into the ark—that is, the church. But we need more than just to be separated outwardly from the evil world. Only the inward renewing and cleansing through the blood and Spirit of Christ can save us from God's eternal wrath. That is the only way to be saved from the judgment that rests on the wicked world.

Luther points this out in his commentary on 1 Peter 3:20-21. This explanation is significant because Luther was the first to introduce this "flood-prayer," known by the early Christian church, into the form for the administration of baptism. He says, "Baptism therefore is a going under of our old nature into death and the resurrection of the new man, who through Christ's blood and Spirit is cleansed and renewed." Luther later concludes, "By using a physical analogy it is possible to briefly express what faith is. But the apostle means to say that what happened when Noah was building the ark also happens today. Just as at that time he, together with seven others, was saved in the ark which floated on the water, so you, too, must be saved in baptism. That water drowned everything that had life. Thus baptism drowns everything that is carnal and natural; it makes spiritual men."

Such a baptism is necessary for each of us for salvation. The outward privilege is not sufficient; in Noah's ark, there still was a mocking Ham. Yet the privilege of baptism is great. It is compared with the entering into the ark while the whole world goes under in the water. But it is a privilege which makes us think of Paul's words, "Lest there be any fornicator, or profane person, as Esau."

Having discussed the first deed of the almighty and eternal God, the prayer mentions the second sign of God's power and says: "Thou, who hast drowned the obstinate Pharaoh and his host in the Red Sea, and hast led thy people Israel through the midst of the Sea upon dry ground." Now the prayer quotes the second wonder: the leading of the Israelites through the Red Sea. And again, the authors say, "By which baptism was signified."

Once again, this is taken from Scripture. The apostle Paul says in 1 Corinthians 10:1-2, "Moreover, brethren, I would not that ye should be ignorant, how that all our fathers were under the cloud, and all passed through the sea; and were all baptized unto Moses in the cloud and in the sea." God's saving of Israel in leading them through the Red Sea was impressive. The Scriptures again and again speak of this almighty and gracious event. Without crossing the Sea, Israel would have been a prey to Pharaoh's murderous claws. But God made Israel a path through the raging waves and deep waters. With the pillar of a cloud as a guide, passing through the Red Sea was to Israel like a baptism by which they were led out from the bondage of the unholy Egypt and brought into the holy Canaan. Through the Red Sea there was a separation between Israel and Egypt; likewise, baptism makes a separation between the church and the world. Once again, it must be said that, though the privilege is great, it is not sufficient for the salvation of the soul. This is biblical; when Paul speaks about the passage of the Israelites through the Red Sea, he adds the following words of warning, "But with many of them God was not well pleased: for they were overthrown in the wilderness." They enjoyed a great privilege. They passed through the Red Sea, and yet they did not enter into Canaan. They fell in the wilderness because they rejected and despised their privileges. They could not enter in because of their unbelief.

To enter into Canaan, they had to not only leave the outward Egypt, but also escape the bondage of sin. The water alone is not sufficient.

The Belgic Confession of Faith says in Article 34, "Not that this is effected by the external water, but by the sprinkling of the precious blood of the Son of God; who is our Red Sea, through which we must pass, to escape the tyranny of Pharaoh, that is, the devil, and to enter into the spiritual land of Canaan." We will enter into Canaan only when, by faith, we have passed through the Red Sea of the blood of Immanuel.

Having quoted these words, it should be evident why the church refers to these things in the prayer. Based on these wonders of God, she pleads for His mercy upon the children of the church. Thus, the prayer continues: "We beseech thee, that Thou wilt be pleased of thine infinite mercy, graciously to look upon these children."

In baptism, the church pleads for God's mercy for the child. The church asks for mercy from that God who showed such great wonders of salvation unto Noah's family and the Israelites. The church, aware of the child's deep misery, pleads for God's great mercy. The prayer calls God's mercy "great." That means, it cannot be measured or comprehended. Great mercy is what God bestowed on Noah's family when they were not destroyed in the flood with the rest of the entire human race, and on miserable Israel in Egypt. His mercy was great; it could not be measured. Pleading on this great mercy, the church asks God to graciously look on the children who receive the sign and seal of baptism.

The praying congregation realizes that the child needs the same mercy that God showed to Noah and Israel. The child is by nature a child of wrath and, like the first world, is condemnable before God. By nature, the child is as evil and depraved as were Pharaoh and the Egyptians. Therefore, only great mercy can save. This is the plea of the congregation when she recommends to God the children who are to be baptized.

But, there is yet another pleading ground in this text. The original text of this prayer says, "This Thy child or these Thy children." This pronoun, "Thy," has been left out of the text by the printers about 300 years ago, but according to the original text it should be included. This little pronoun has great significance. The child, on whose behalf the church prays, is born within the bounds of the covenant. For this reason, God calls the child to be baptized His child. We see this very clearly in Ezekiel 16:21, "That thou hast slain my children, and delivered

them to cause them to pass through the fire for them?" According-
ing to the covenant relationship in which their seed was
included, the Lord calls the children of the Israelites "My children." For the same reason, the Lord calls the entire people of
Israel "His people." If God calls the children of the old
covenant His, how much more are the children of the new
covenant His people? This covenant, being greater than that of
the Old Testament, now includes the whole visible church.

However, we may not interpret the word "Thy" to apply to
inward grace. This is not the intent. The church may not deter-
mine this for she does not know the things God has hidden from
us. If the form considered this to mean the inward state, then
there would be no point in praying for God to "graciously look
upon these children." No, the form uses the words "Thy child"
because of the covenant relationship; it is used as a pleading
ground. By saying, "This Thy child," the congregation reminds
God of the covenant which He made with her and her seed.

"Thy child" means the child who was separated by God
from the world as He separated Noah from the first world and
Israel from the heathen. The child belongs to the assembly that
God calls "holy." The church asks God to be gracious to the
child whom He has separated from the world through baptism.
Because the child is born in the visible church and bears the sign
of the covenant of grace, God has a special right to this child.
The child is in duty bound to serve God and to obey Him.

Therefore, the Lord says concerning the children of the
Israelites, "Moreover thou hast taken thy sons and thy daughters, whom thou hast borne unto me, and these hast thou
sacrificed." Regarding the words "borne unto me," the Dutch
annotations say, "That is, who belonged to me by virtue of the
covenant which I made with you and your seed. Even though
the Jewish people had forsaken God, and were worthy of being
forsaken by God, nevertheless, as this had not happened yet, it
generated children, whom He through circumcision considered
to be His, not desiring to punish the children for the transgression of the parents. Likewise Ezekiel 23:37." These words speak

for themselves. The children of the Israelites belonged to God by virtue of the covenant, and likewise, baptized children now belong to God. On this privilege the church pleads for God to graciously look upon these children.

The church asks the Lord "graciously to look upon...." She calls for grace for her children. A church that understands baptism cannot do otherwise. The thought of the child's misery makes her call out for grace. It is the prayer of the publican, "Oh God, be merciful to me and my children, sinners!"

Incorporation into Christ
The next thing the church prays for is incorporation into Christ. This follows the prayer for mercy. The church realizes that only those who are in Christ are delivered from God's severe and just judgment. Therefore, the congregation prays, "And incorporate them by thy Holy Spirit, into thy Son Jesus Christ, that they may be buried with him into his death and be raised with him in newness of life."

The congregation asks that the child, who will be baptized, be incorporated into Christ, the Head of the covenant of grace. It is of utmost importance for each fallen sinner, who by nature is in Adam, that he be incorporated into Christ through a true faith. Being in Adam brings the just punishment and eternal judgment of God on us; only our belonging to Christ can bring us blessing and eternal life. All our misery comes from Adam and all our happiness comes from Christ. Therefore, the church not only prays for an outward union with Christ through baptism, but for an inward union with Christ through renewal by the Holy Spirit. Only when the sinner is united with Christ by a true faith will he share in Christ's benefits.

This clearly shows that the authors did not consider all children to be born again, although some accuse the authors of this. By a judgment of charity, our Reformed fathers made positive assumptions about children who died at a young age. They confessed that we should not think too little of God's mercy, of baptism, and of the prayers of the church at baptism. You can find this in the Canons of Dort and in the minutes of the Synod of 1618-1619. Yet, despite this trust in God's mercy, they understood very clearly that it was necessary for baptized children to be incorporated into Christ by the Holy Spirit in order to be saved.

This is what the praying congregation asks for their children: "that they may be buried with him into his death and be raised with him in newness of life." These words describe the true spiritual meaning of baptism. True baptism is burial with Christ in order to later rise in newness of life with Christ. Once again, this is a biblical citation. In Romans 6:4 the apostle says, "Therefore we are buried with him by baptism into death: that like as Christ was raised up from the dead by the glory of the Father, even so we also should walk in newness of life."

Baptism pictures the relationship between Christ's death and His resurrection. It is a burial of the old life of sin, to rise again to a new and better life with Christ in the power of His resurrection. The old life has been put off and buried with Christ; the new life has been put on to the glory of God in conformity with Christ.

The text of Romans 6:4 and the authors' citation of it should be read in the context of the practice by the early Christian church to baptize by immersion. The person being baptized first was "buried" in the water and then rose from the water. The old heathen life, the old man of sin, was buried; the new man, the Christian, rose from the water. This was to be baptized in its truest sense.

The church asks for this true baptism for the child. The church asks God to make baptism for the child a burial and rising with Christ. Baptism is a sacrament of birth: a birth of water and Spirit. As the congregation realizes that this new birth is necessary for this child, they ask that its baptism would be more than an outward sign; they pray that it would be a sign of a new birth.

The congregation desires that this baptized child be one who will walk in newness of life and who will truly be dedicated to the Lord. The congregation knows that this will only be the case when the child is spiritually buried and raised with Christ. Only then will the sinner be a new man. Only communion with Christ, the efficacy of His death, and the power of His resurrection can work this.

"May daily follow him, joyfully bearing their cross, and cleave unto him in true faith, firm hope, and ardent love." In this prayer, the form considers that the children being baptized will encounter crosses and difficulties. From the Scriptures, the congregation knows what can befall us in this life. They know that sin subjects us to many troubles and afflictions. They do not ask for the crosses to be taken away from the children, but for these crosses to be sanctified. They ask God to give them what is necessary—that is, grace—to bear their crosses and thus to follow Christ. The bearing of the cross is associated with the true discipleship of Jesus Christ. The Lord Jesus said, "And whosoever doth not bear his cross, and come after me, cannot be my disciple" (Luke 14:27). If the prayer for the children to be incorporated into Christ is heard, the children must take up their cross and follow Jesus as true disciples.

In the prayer, the congregation asks for the special grace required for this self-denial. How applicable were these words, particularly when this form was written. True disciples of Christ were persecuted, robbed of their possessions, and sometimes were even put to death. They truly became cross-bearers.

Everyone has crosses to bear, but for those who are truly united with Christ by faith, there are special crosses. Union with Christ brings with it a share in His reproach and cross. Here below, the church of God walks on a road of the cross because of the battle with her three mortal enemies: the devil, the world, and her own sinful flesh. Only gradually will the old man die away and the new man be raised up.

Therefore, the congregation prays that the children may "joyfully" bear their crosses. This may sound strange to us, since we seldom associate joy and cross-bearing together. But this is not strange in the life of faith. The true Christian is comforted under his cross. When he bears his cross, following Jesus, he will find joy and comfort in cross-bearing. It is said of Christ, "Who for the joy that was set before him endured the cross, despising the shame" (Acts 12:2). When we carry our cross with our eyes on Christ, we can sing with Paul and Silas in the prison and understand the words of Jesus, "Blessed are ye, when men shall revile you, and persecute you, and shall say all manner of evil against you falsely, for my sake. Rejoice, and be exceeding glad: for great is your reward in heaven: for so persecuted they the prophets which were before you" (Matt. 5:11-12). It is a Christian's honor to bear the cross of Jesus; it makes the disciple like his Master. Therefore, the congregation prays that the baptized child will "daily follow Him." We must follow in Jesus' footsteps. This is what Peter says, "For even hereunto were ye called: because Christ also suffered for us, leaving us an example, that ye should follow his steps" (1 Pet. 2:21). To bear the name "Christian" is to be conformed to the Master, to take up the cross daily, and to follow Him.

"And cleave unto him in true faith, firm hope, and ardent love." The congregation prays for more for the children. They ask the God of the covenant that the children may not only be joined to Him with an outward bond of baptism, but with an inward bond of faith, hope, and love. A three-fold cord is mentioned—a cord that will not and cannot be easily broken. We recognize Paul's conclusion: "And now abideth faith, hope, charity, these three" (1 Cor. 13:13). This cord binds all true believers to Christ, their Lord and Savior. Many branches are joined to Christ, the Vine, by the outward ties of baptism, profession, and church membership, but true branches are joined to Christ by this three-fold cord of faith, hope, and love.

The congregation prays for this bond with Christ for the children being baptized. They desire these baptized children to have communion with Christ not only as outward branches, but to be joined to Christ with the unbreakable bonds of faith, hope, and love.

"With a comfortable sense of thy favor, leave this life, which is nothing but a continual death, and at the last day, may appear without terror before the judgment seat of Christ thy Son." The congregation prays God for all things necessary for life and salvation for the children, but their prayer also considers life's end. They want the children to look beyond this life and to fix their eyes on its end. They want to impress on the children the eternal future that lies beyond all of our lives. We must all appear before the judgment seat of Christ.

The child has just been born. Yet the authors of the form understand that this newborn child will also have to leave this life. Life is viewed in light of eternity. Everything will end in eternity, and this applies to the newborn child, too. Therefore, the congregation prays that the child may leave this life with a comfortable sense of God's favor.

The authors of the form say that this life is nothing else but a continual death. This may be gloomy language, but it is biblical language. According to God's Word, this life has become a continual death because of sin. The sentence over the life of fallen man is this: "In the day that thou eatest thereof thou shalt surely die." Literally, it says, "dying thou shalt die." We are born to die; life is a candlestick that burns up. Today we lose our health, tomorrow our prosperity, then our spouses, and finally we die ourselves.

The Reformers did not despise life, but neither did they glorify it. They saw the shadow of death spread out over our entire lives. Knowing this, the believer sets his desires on eternal life rather than upon this life. Likewise, the congregation prays that when death comes for these children, God will allow them to leave this life with comfort, and for the sake of Christ's righteousness, appear without terror before the judgment seat of God.

Christ's judgment seat is the destination of each one of us. According to God's Word, we all must appear before that judgment seat. The authors did not forget about the second coming of Christ; He shall come again to judge the quick and the dead. The child at some time will stand before God's judgment seat.

As the parents now stand with their children before the baptismal font, so they will one day stand with their children before the judgment seat of Christ. We should bear this in mind when we answer "Yes" to the baptismal questions. One day, our word will come back to us. How terrible it would be to bring our children into the church to be baptized and never speak even one word to them about their salvation. Consider this! Our journey, and that of our children, is to the judgment seat of Christ. Can you justify bringing your children up with only worldly pleasures? We should fear that the Lord would then say of us what He said of the Israelites, "That thou hast slain my children, and delivered them to cause them to pass through the fire for them" (Ezek. 16:21). Israel sacrificed their children to the Moloch, and that is what we also do when we sacrifice them to this world and do not bring them up in the fear of the Lord. Parents, take this to heart! We travel with our children to the judgment seat of Jesus Christ.

How many baptized children break with God and His Word when they grow older! There is a terrible danger of stirring up the wrath of the Lamb among those who are baptized. Truly, there is much reason to pray for the children of the kingdom that one day they may appear without terror before the judgment seat of Christ. To these disobedient children, the following words apply, "Which knew his lord's will, and prepared not himself, neither did according to his will, shall be beaten with many stripes" (Luke 12:47). The children of the covenant are those who know the way; they know that there is a Name given under heaven for salvation. They are acquainted with the gospel of Christ. How great is the responsibility to be baptized and to know the way. Therefore, today, when you hear His voice, harden not your hearts.

"Through Jesus Christ our Lord, who with thee and the Holy Ghost, one only God, lives and reigns forever. Amen." All that the church has prayed for is asked in the name of Jesus Christ. The congregation understands Christ's words that "whatsoever ye shall ask the Father in my name, he will give it you." Unworthy and guilty in ourselves, Christ must be the only ground of our prayer. Thus the authors of the form lead the congregation to finish praying with the words "for Jesus' sake."

No blessing will ever be granted to us because of something in ourselves. The congregation lays this petition on the altar of Christ's merits and calls on the triune God: "who with thee and the Holy Ghost, one only God, lives and reigns forever. Amen." The triune God is the God of baptism, and in just a moment the child will be baptized in His name. In worship, the congregation ends the prayer to the triune God by confessing that He lives and reigns forever.

CHAPTER 4

The Exhortation to the Parents

The Baptismal Questions

At the administration of baptism, the church asks the parents certain questions in the name of God. The parents are to answer these questions affirmatively before God and the congregation. The custom to ask such questions is very old and has a biblical basis; both John the Baptist and the apostles did this before they administered baptism. Furthermore, the early Christian church had the custom of questioning the people being baptized before administering baptism. This was known as "baptismal questioning."

Tertullian and Cyprian wrote about this baptismal questioning. The person to be baptized was asked, "Do you renounce Satan?" The person answered, "I do." Then he was asked, "Do you assent to Christ?" The person said, "I do." After answering these questions, he was baptized to bear the mark of Christ. No one was ever baptized without doing confession of faith.

It is true that infant baptism concerns a child that is not yet capable of reasoning. Yet, baptism is not administered to this child without asking the parents, or guardians, the baptismal questions, which are as follows.

An Exhortation to the Parents[3]
Beloved in the Lord Jesus Christ, you have heard that baptism is an

---

[2] The heading in the Dutch form reads, "An exhortation to the parents and the witnesses." We should keep this in mind when reading the sections that discuss this heading.

ordinance of God, to seal unto us and to our seed his covenant; therefore it must be used for that end, and not out of custom or superstition. That it may then be manifest, that you are thus minded, you are to answer sincerely to these questions:

First. Whether you acknowledge, that although our children are conceived and born in sin, and therefore are subject to all miseries, yea, to condemnation itself; yet that they are sanctified in Christ, and therefore, as members of his Church ought to be baptized?

Secondly. Whether you acknowledge the doctrine which is contained in the Old and New Testament, and in the articles of the Christian faith, and which is taught here in this Christian Church, to be the true and perfect doctrine of salvation?

Thirdly. Whether you promise and intend to see these children, when come to the years of discretion (whereof you are either parent or witness), instructed and brought up in the aforesaid doctrine, or help or cause them to be instructed therein, to the utmost of your power?

Answer. Yes.

These questions were drawn up by Peter Datheen. We said before that the rest of the form was copied by à Lasco and Zwingli, and from the school at Heidelberg in Paltz, Germany. These questions, however, are characteristic of Datheen. Although they are somewhat similar to those of à Lasco, the differences are apparent enough to indicate that Datheen drew them up himself. To prove this, we will reproduce à Lasco's questions, which will also be useful to understand how the fugitive congregation in London, cooperating closely with Calvin, baptized children. The questions are as follows:

I desire that you declare:

1. Whether these children, which you have brought hither, are the seed of our church, so that they may be legitimately baptized here through our ministration?

2. Do you acknowledge our doctrine, which you have heard concerning baptism and its mysteries, to be true and that our children by nature are children of wrath and death, like we ourselves are, but who are now comprehended with us in the divine covenant for Christ's sake, and upon Christ's command, are to be sealed with the seal of acceptance (that is, with baptism) of His righteousness?

3. Finally, do you acknowledge that it is your solemn duty, as
well as that of the entire church, but in particular of you
fathers with your wives, the mothers of the children, that you
will have your children, which are brought hither, instructed
in the true knowledge and service of God when they come to
the years of discretion?

We see that these questions differ substantially from our
form, although in essence the parents are asked the same things.
It will be useful for us to come back to this later.

The heading reads: "An exhortation to the parents and
those who witness." The exhortation is directed to the baptismal
parents and to other people present. The parents stand here as
both members of the church and instructors of their children.
The witnesses are the so-called godfathers and godmothers. We
will discuss this later when we deal with the last question.

The opening words begin thus: "Beloved in the Lord Jesus
Christ." The authors follow the example of the apostles who
address their letters likewise. This does not mean that the apostles considered each member of the congregation to be truly
saved; from their letters it is abundantly clear that they were well
aware of the fact that there was chaff among the wheat. Rather,
they addressed the congregation this way because she was a visible revelation of the congregation of Jesus Christ. The church
is more than a religious association. She is the body of Jesus
Christ even though there are hypocrites among her. The members of the church are called Christians according to their
confession and are therefore addressed as beloved in the Lord
Jesus Christ. The Lord Jesus called Judas a "friend" and the
hardened Jews "children of the kingdom"; similarly, Peter
repeatedly called the Jews "brethren." Only God knows who are
real members of Christ's body.

Next, a short summary points out the scriptural content of
baptism: "you have heard that baptism is an ordinance of God,
to seal unto us and to our seed his covenant." From what was
read to them, the parents heard what baptism is and what purpose it serves. First, baptism is an institution of God, not of

man. It originates from God. Under the Old Testament, God granted circumcision to the nation of Israel; under the New Testament, He granted the seal of baptism to the visible church.

Why did the Lord give these institutions? "To seal unto us and to our seed his covenant." This is a clear and short description of baptism. Baptism serves to seal God's covenant. This is the primary basis of infant baptism. Baptism neither primarily concerns the faith of the parents or children, nor a presupposed regeneration of the children, but the confirmation of God's covenant. The children of the visible members of the church are baptized not because they have faith or because faith is presupposed in them, but because they belong to the holy bond of God's covenant. Baptism does the same as circumcision did under the Old Testament—it seals the truth of God's covenant and His words. Therefore, God's covenant and promises are the only ground for baptism.

We have already elaborated on God's promise to Abraham and what it means that God seals His covenant to us and to our children. This gives hope for the future generations. Rev. Kersten said as follows:

> God's covenant and promises are sealed in Holy Baptism, although baptism is administered to children (like Ishmael and Esau) who shall never inherit salvation, because they are vessels of wrath fitted to destruction (Rom. 9:22). In that knowledge lies the liberty to baptize little children, to ask and answer the questions, and to call upon the Lord in prayer and thanksgiving, as the form for the administration of baptism prescribes. But then presupposed regeneration, as a ground for infant baptism, falls away as sand from under our feet. Thus baptism remains a sign and seal that the Lord remembers His covenant forever; that He will be our God and the God of our seed to a thousand generations, according to His good pleasure, not always glorifying His grace from parent to child, but gathering His elect out of the natural generations to one spiritual generation, in which the great covenant grace of salvation is confirmed, "I shall be their God and they shall be my people" (*Reformed Dogmatics*, p. 517).

From this follows "therefore it must be used for that end, and not out of custom or superstition." We must use baptism for the purpose given by God—namely, to seal His covenant to us and to our children. Therefore, baptism may not be used out of custom or superstition.

"Not out of custom." We can baptize out of routine, simply because this is "what is done." We do it as a matter of course, without even thinking about it. Soon we go to the church out of habit, pray and read out of custom, without even thinking about it. This is the case for many parents and even for whole congregations. Some people are interested only in whether the child is nicely dressed, whether the child has a nice christening robe, who brings it into the church, etc. Others consider the administration of baptism a disruption of the service. "A baptismal service again!" they say. "The administration of baptism prolongs the service and we only get half a sermon." To these, the words of the Lord Jesus apply, "So then because thou art lukewarm, and neither cold nor hot, I will spue thee out of my mouth" (Rev. 3:16). Let us be careful and fearful of a sinful routine and lukewarm customary service.

"And not out of superstition." With this the authors thought in particular of the Roman Catholic Church, whose superstition makes the baptismal waters a means of grace. They teach that the sacrament effects grace in the person being baptized; a kind of magical power is in the water of baptism.

However, our hearts are sometimes just as popish as the Roman Catholic doctrine. We say with Israel, "We are Abraham's children; we are baptized; we have the ark in our midst," while the God of Abraham and the Christ of the ark have no value to us. Then baptism is used as a pillow on which we sleep a spiritual sleep of death.

Baptism may not be used out of custom or superstition. Baptism must be used with faith; whatever is not of faith is sin. This sacrament must be administered to God's honor, our comfort, and the edification of the church. Then baptism will receive its proper place—namely, to confirm God's covenant to our downcast hearts.

"That it then may be manifest, that you are thus minded, you are to answer sincerely to these questions." The officebearer baptizes the child in the Name of Christ. He is responsible for the manner in which he administers baptism; the parents are responsible for the manner in which they answer the questions. The church does not give the answers for them. They are to give the answers themselves and make a vow before the eyes of the living and all-knowing God. They have to answer sincerely. The parents do not just stand before the minister or the congregation, but before God, who tries the reins and the heart. This should be experienced more, primarily by the parents, but also by the congregation, and in particular, by the officebearers. We answer the questions *pro Deo*—that is, before God.

We are not to inquire into the condition of the parents' hearts when they bring their child to baptism. We must urge for hearts that are sincere before God, but the responsibility for the answer lies with the parents, not with the church. The church can only apply discipline over the doctrine and the public walk of life; it is not to judge the hearts.

The parents are responsible for raising their children in the fear of God. If they do not act according to the affirmative answer given, then they, not the church who asked the questions, will be accountable to God.

The First Baptismal Question

First. Whether you acknowledge, that although our children are conceived and born in sin, and therefore are subject to all miseries, yea, to condemnation itself; yet that they are sanctified in Christ, and therefore, as members of his Church ought to be baptized?

The key point of this question is that the children ought to be baptized, and the authors give the reason why. The question first confronts us with the condition of sin and misery to which all mankind is subject through Adam's fall. Because of sin, we are subject to all miseries, even to condemnation itself.

Although this applies to everyone, this question particularly concerns the children to be baptized.

Both the parents and the congregation are told what kind of children are baptized: they are children of wrath. The children do not possess personal grace or a presupposed regeneration, but they are fallen creatures. They are conceived and born in sin. The gate through which we enter natural life is sinful. Consequently, the children are subject to all manner of miseries and the just punishments of God.

But, the question continues, although our children are thus by nature, do you acknowledge that they are yet "sanctified in Christ, and therefore, as members of his church ought to be baptized?"

At first glance, it would seem difficult to answer this question with "Yes." This difficulty arises from incorrectly understanding both the authors of the form and the synods that always supported this question. If we understand the words "sanctified in Christ" to mean inward sanctification, it is indeed impossible for parents to answer "Yes." The parents cannot know whether their children are in Christ and partakers of the inward sanctification of the Spirit. How then could parents confirm that their children are inwardly holy?

The authors do not speak about subjective inward holiness, but about outward holiness through the covenant. "Covenant holiness" is what is meant. Because this is not understood, people are anxious about answering this question positively. But the authors saw the connection between the Old Testament nation of Israel and the visible church of the New Testament; Israel was called a holy congregation, and so the church of the New Testament is a holy congregation—not in the sense of inward holiness and sanctification, but in the sense of being separated from the world. Only when we keep this in mind can we understand their statements about the seed of the visible church.

If parents do not understand this properly, then they cannot give a positive answer, and we bring those who fear the Lord into great difficulty. Fruytier says this on the issue:

This question often causes much anxiety in the hearts of those who fear God, because the parents are not asked, whether their children must *become* sanctified, but whether in Christ they *are already* sanctified. And therefore some judge that it were better to ask, "Do you not believe that your children, being sanctified in Christ, ought to be baptized?" Or, "Do you not believe that your children must only be sanctified in Christ and therefore ought to be baptized?" Or, "That there are children who are sanctified in Christ and therefore ought to be baptized?" This anxiety is caused by this: that many judge that the authors of the form only seem to have in mind a true sanctification through Jesus' blood and Spirit. But it is often observed that in their growing up even children of the most godly parents turn out to be true children of Belial, such as were, under the circumcision, the two ungodly sons of the godly Eli (*The Great Privilege of Children of Christians*, p. 136).

Fruytier points out that for this reason some have tried to change the questions because they understood the words "are sanctified in Christ" to mean true inward sanctification. But such an inward sanctification is not intended here. We must point out that we are not allowed to change the question or to add to it. We should respect the form for the administration of baptism. Many have inserted the word "some" and read, "Do you not believe that *some* children are sanctified in Christ." Others have inserted the word "can": "Whether they *can* be sanctified in Christ." This is wrong; we ought to do justice to the authors and convey their own words. Linguistically, it concerns children and parents who have come to the baptism and is addressed to the parents, who now stand before the baptismal font. It concerns their children, who were said to be subject to condemnation; these same children are now said to be sanctified in Christ. It is a misconception to state that the form concerns the essence of the church. It concerns these parents and their children. None of the Reformed fathers ever dared, nor wanted, to change the forms. Comrie says, "Without reading the questions as they are worded, I would never baptize" (*Heidelberg*

Catechism, p. 123). The form is written for the members of the visible church, not just for converted parents.

All these things have come about because people have interpreted the words "are sanctified in Christ" incorrectly. If we interpret these words to mean inner sanctification, we either have to change the wording or affirm presupposed regeneration, like Abraham Kuyper. Remember that, based on an interpretation of inner sanctification, the Synod of the Reformed Churches in 1905 proposed the following, "And concerning the fourth point—the supposed regeneration—your synod declares that in accordance with the confession of our churches the seed of the covenant, according to the promise of God, is to be seen as regenerated and sanctified in Christ, until the opposite is shown in their life through their conduct or doctrine." This statement is one of the consequences of interpreting the words "are sanctified in Christ" to mean an inner sanctification.

Baptism is not a seal and sign of regeneration, but rather a sign and seal of God's covenant and promises. Therefore, we should study the word "sanctification" thoroughly in order to understand its true meaning.

The original meaning of this word in the Bible is to cut, to separate, and to set apart. All translators say that the stem of the Hebrew word can best be translated as "to set apart." Its actual connotation is "to belong to a different category"; thus, God is "holy." He belongs to a different category. He alone is God, the Holy One of Israel.

When we read the word "holy" in the Bible, it means to set apart from that which is common or unclean. So we read in the Scriptures of the sanctification of people, times, places, and items. The priests were sanctified, the Sabbath and the great Day of Atonement were sanctified, the places of Shiloh and Jerusalem were sanctified, and the instruments of the tabernacle and the temple were also called holy. These were separated for the service of God.

Now the same thing is said of the whole nation of Israel. The visible church of the Jews, children included, are called holy: "And ye shall be unto me a kingdom of priests, and an holy nation" (Ex. 19:6); "For thou art an holy people unto the Lord thy God" (Deut. 7:6). See also Deuteronomy 14:2, 26:19, and Daniel 8:24. In contrast, the Gentiles, who were outside of Israel, are called unholy: "For henceforth there shall no more come into thee the uncircumcised and the unclean" (Isa. 52:1); "It is not meet to take the children's bread, and to cast it to dogs" (Matt. 15:26); "We who are Jews by nature, and not sinners of the Gentiles" (Gal. 2:15). The children of the visible church are called "the holy seed" (Ezra 9:2), "my children, whom thou hast borne unto me" (Ezek. 16:21), "a godly seed" (Mal. 2:15), "children of the kingdom" (Matt. 8:12), and "children of the covenant" (Acts 3:25).

These texts do not concern an inward sanctification, but rather an outward sanctification—a separation from the world. The apostle says in 1 Corinthians 7:14, "Else were your children unclean; but now are they holy." The Dutch annotations say, "That is, the children are comprehended in the external covenant of God and have access to the marks and seals of God's grace." The Scriptures are clear: the words "holy" and "sanctify" mean "to separate" or "to set apart." It is covenantal sanctification, not an inward regeneration.

We will now consider how our Reformed fathers interpreted the word "holy" as regards the seed of the church. First we will consider the great Reformer, Calvin, who says in his commentary on 1 Corinthians 7:14,

> The passage, then, teaches that the children of the pious are set apart from others by a sort of exclusive privilege, so as to be reckoned holy in the Church. But how will this statement correspond with what he teaches elsewhere—that we are all by nature children of wrath (Eph. 2:3); or with the statement of David—Behold I was conceived in sin, etc. (Ps. 51:7). I answer, that there is a universal propagation of sin and damnation throughout the seed of Adam, and all, therefore, to a man, are included in this curse, whether they are the off-spring of believers or of the ungodly; for it is not as regenerated by the Spirit, that believers beget children after

the flesh. The natural condition, therefore, of all is alike, so that they are liable equally to sin and to eternal death. As to the Apostle's assigning here a peculiar privilege to the children of believers, this flows from the blessing of the covenant, by the intervention of which the curse of nature is removed; and those who were by nature unholy are consecrated to God by grace. Hence Paul argues, in his Epistle to the Romans (11:16), that the whole of Abraham's posterity are holy, because God had made a covenant of life with him—if the root be holy, says he, then the branches are holy also. And God calls all that were descended from Israel his sons: now that the partition is broken down, the same covenant of salvation that was entered into with the seed of Abraham is communicated to us. But if the children of believers are exempted from the common lot of mankind, so as to be set apart to the Lord, why should we keep them back from the sign? If the Lord admits them into the church by his word, why should we refuse them the sign? In what respects the offspring of the pious are holy, while many of them degenerate, you will find explained in the tenth and eleventh chapters of the Epistle to the Romans.

I assume that everyone will understand what Calvin means. Because of the covenant relationship, Israel was called holy, and the children of the New Testament church were called a holy generation. At the end of this portion, Calvin points out that many become degenerate. We will discuss this in more detail later. That which is called a holy generation outwardly is not necessarily holy inwardly.

Being sanctified in Christ means a separation from the common lot of the human race and being brought within the boundaries of the covenant. Israel was a holy nation. In His sovereign good pleasure, He chose them out of all nations to know His covenant and words. "He hath not dealt so with any nation: and as for his judgments, they have not known them" (Ps. 147:20); "In times past He suffered all nations to walk in their own ways" (Acts 14:16); "They were strangers from the covenants of promise" (Eph. 2:12).

Even today, God has the gospel preached to only a certain part of the Gentiles. Is it not a small number that knows the pure message of the gospel? God's messengers have not yet been sent to many to pray them in Christ's stead, "Be ye reconciled unto God." But the children of the visible church are brought into a congregation, which is called holy. They are born under the administration of the gospel. "Else were your children unclean; but now are they holy" (1 Cor. 7:14).

The words "are sanctified in Christ" point, therefore, to an outward sanctification or separation. This is also the meaning of the word "sanctified" when it refers to the children of the visible church. It does not mean regenerate or elect, but sanctified through the covenant. The promise of the covenant previously rested on the Israelite children but now rests on the children of the visible church.

Fruytier points out that this is what our fathers meant with this question.

> Further confirmation—that the church believes in such an outward sanctification through the covenant—may be obtained if we observe the petition for the baptismal children of the visible church. Following upon the two grounds mentioned in the beginning, the prayer continues: *We beseech Thee, that Thou wilt be pleased of thine infinite mercy, graciously to look upon these children, and incorporate them by thy Holy Spirit, into thy Son Jesus Christ, etc.* If the church did not acknowledge an outward sanctification through the covenant, but viewed all baptized children as inwardly sanctified, she would not have to pray for God to graciously look upon them and to incorporate them into Christ. She would only need to thank God that they were incorporated into Christ. This, however, is not done, but the petition is that God incorporates them into Christ (*The Great Privilege of Children of Christians*, p. 148).

God's covenant promises are for the children of the church. This is what the parents are asked to acknowledge. On the one hand, they are asked to acknowledge that their children are children of wrath; but, on the other hand, they are asked to acknowledge that, even though their children are children of wrath like any other child, nevertheless, the Lord has graciously separated them from the world. Calvin says emphatically, "Wherefore, both the children of the Jews, because, when made heirs of that covenant, they were separated from the heathen, were called a holy seed, and for the same reason the children of Christians, or those who have only one believing parent, are called holy, and, by the testimony of the apostle (1 Cor. 7:14) differ from the impure seed of idolaters" (*Institutes*, 4.16).

When we consider that Peter Datheen was a Calvinist, we can understand what he meant by this question. The parents were to profess an outward, not an inward, covenant sanctification. They were to profess that, although their children were children of wrath, yet the children of the church were separated and sanctified by God.

Note the apparent contradiction: children of wrath by nature, but sanctified because of God's covenant. The children are separated from the multitude of unbelievers, and that is why they ought to be baptized. This relationship to God's covenant is the only reason for the children to be baptized as members of His church. The promise of God made unto the visible church sanctifies them. The promises of God are for them as they were previously for Abraham's seed.

Thus, the ground of infant baptism is neither that the children are perhaps elect nor that they possibly possess some amount of grace and regeneration. Rather, the basis of infant baptism is the covenant of God to which they belong and through which they are sanctified. The parents are therefore asked whether they acknowledge that, although their children are children of wrath by nature, they nevertheless are sanctified in Christ because of the promise of God made to the children of the church, and therefore as members of His church ought to be baptized.

This agrees with the manner in which the Calvinist refugees in London baptized their children. They said: "Our children by nature are children of wrath and of death, like we ourselves are, but are now included with us in the divine covenant for Christ's sake, and upon Christ's command are surely to be sealed with the seal of acceptance of His righteousness, that is, by baptism."

So, our conclusion about the first question is that we do not need to have studied dogmatics to be able to humbly answer this question with a heartfelt "Yes." We profess with this "Yes" that our children are not children of non-Christian families, but that they are sanctified and separated children. We humbly profess an undeserved privilege given by God to us and to our children, and pray that this covenant God will make these children be true children of God under our only Teacher, King, and High Priest, Jesus Christ, and that they may manfully fight against and overcome sin, the devil, and his whole dominion, to eternally praise and magnify the triune God.

Two Kinds of Covenant Children
Scripture says of many of the covenant nation of Israel, who had been led out of Egypt in such a wonderful way and with whom God had made His covenant, that "God was not well pleased." It was not all Israel that was called Israel. Abraham's sons were of two different types. Upon God's command, Abraham circumcised all who belonged to his house, including Ishmael, his son. Nevertheless, Ishmael was not a believer. Actually, he and his posterity drifted away from God and from the precepts of His covenant. Esau was no different. He also was circumcised and bore the sign of God's covenant, but he placed himself and his posterity outside of the communion of the church by despising the blessing.

What was evident in Israel is also evident in the New Testament church. Shortly after the day of Pentecost, hypocrites became apparent among those that had been baptized. Think of Ananias and Sapphira, Simon the sorcerer, and others. God's church is a church in which chaff and wheat are mixed together. This is a Scriptural truth. Not all those who have made confession of faith and go to the Lord's Supper are true partakers of the covenant; many approach unto the Lord with their lips, but their heart remains far from Him. There were two kinds of Israelites and there were two kinds of children of Abraham. There is a carnal seed and a spiritual seed.

We must believe this when we express the great privilege of our children and say that they are sanctified in Christ. Calvin says in his commentary on Genesis 17:7,

> Here, then, a twofold class of sons presents itself to us, in the Church; for since the whole body of the people is gathered together in the fold of God, by one and the same voice, all without exception, are, in this respect, accounted children; the name of the Church is applicable in common to them all: but in the innermost sanctuary of God, none others are reckoned the sons of God, than they in whom the promise is ratified by faith. And although this difference flows from the fountain of gratuitous election, whence also faith itself springs; yet, since the counsel of God is in itself hidden from us, we therefore distinguish the true from the spurious children, by the respective marks of faith and unbelief.

Thus, Calvin distinguishes in the body of the church two kinds of children.

There is only one covenant of grace, but there are two aspects to this covenant: an inward and an outward aspect. You find this in the Dutch annotations. For example, the marginal notes commenting on 1 Corinthians 7:14 say, "That is, the children are comprehended in the external covenant of God and have access to the signs and seals of God's grace." Furthermore, Franciscus Gomarus says in proposition 31 of his disputation on the sacraments, "The external covenant consists of an outward union with God and the visible church militant upon earth, whereby one separates oneself from the ungodliness and uncleanness of this world by an outward confession of faith and walk of life, and joins oneself to the visible church and the service of God, whilst God acknowledges one to be an outward member of His visible church and in this regard accepts one as being sanctified and a partaker of the covenant." He then continues in proposition 32, "And in this manner God calls Himself in general the God of the visible church and calls her His people, and kingdom, and children of the kingdom, even though darnel is mixed with wheat. And so the hypocrites, although they lack true faith, are comprehended with the true believers in the same external community, which is striving under God's banner."

This involves one covenant with two aspects—not two covenants. Jacobus Koelman teaches this in his work against the Labadists: "The covenant is one, but all are not comprehended in the covenant in the same manner. Some are only comprehended in the covenant by an outward confession and, as present partakers, enjoy the outward privileges. But, some are comprehended through a sincere acceptance of the covenant, and these enjoy the saving benefits by means of these privileges" (*The Error of the Labadists*, p. 566).

Brakel only speaks of an "outward acceptance into the covenant," whereas Olevianus says, "This covenant should be considered in a two-fold manner. First, the essence of the covenant, or the things that are promised by God. Secondly, concerning its administration in the visible church" (*Covenant of Grace*, p. 2). Johannes Appelius says:

> This covenant has an inward and an outward form. The inward form consists of a spiritual, true and voluntary dealing and covenanting between God and the sinner. The outward form consists of an outward profession and confirmation of the inward covenant through the Word, sacraments, profession, and conduct. But this does not mean that there are two distinct covenants—one internal and one external—even though the covenant of grace could be called an inward covenant concerning its inward form and an outward covenant concerning its outward form. It is but one and the same spiritual covenant of grace, like the inward and outward man is but one and the same man" (*Principle Foundation of the Sacraments*, p. 92).

These citations are sufficient proof of the fact that there is nothing new in stating that the covenant of grace consists in having two sides—that is, the essence and the administration of the covenant. Many are included in the administration of the covenant who are not partakers of the essence of the covenant. We must not lose sight of this. There is a great privilege in being outwardly associated with this covenant, but being personally included in the covenant through repentance and faith is necessary for salvation.

In the parable of the vine and the branches, the Lord Jesus taught the difference between being related to Him in an inward or outward manner. It is possible to be a branch of Him and yet to be burned. Calvin says in his commentary on John 15:2, "But here comes a question, Can any one who is engrafted into Christ be without fruit? I answer, many are supposed to be *in the vine*, according to the opinion of men, who actually have no root *in the vine*. Thus, in the writings of the prophets, the Lord calls the people of Israel *his vine*, because, by outward profession, they had the name of the Church."

To be truly a fruit-bearing branch, it is necessary to be incorporated in Christ through regeneration. Those who are baptized but do not bring forth fruits of faith and repentance will be hewn off and cast into the fire. If God did not spare the Jews, the natural branches, because of their hard hearts and rejection of the salvation He offered, then He will certainly not spare the unnatural branches. They will also be hewn off because of their unbelief. We can have a certain relationship with Christ through baptism and an outward confession of faith, and yet in the end be burnt with fire. Yes, we can even have the gifts of the Holy Spirit, and taste the power of the kingdom to come, and yet not live out of the Vine — that is, Christ (Heb. 6).

However, God's promises in baptism are certain and faithful. We may not undervalue the covenant. The fact that there is a distinction between the two kinds of children of the covenant may not lead us to think that baptism is but a sign of an external covenant privilege. The sacraments are not signs of external blessings only, but signs and seals of God's covenant and of the promises of eternal blessing.

There is only one covenant of grace. We acknowledge that

there is a tension between the covenant privileges and eternal election, but we may not solve this by splitting the covenant into two covenants: an internal and an external one. Neither may we make a distinction in the offer of grace and say that there is a genuine offer to the elect, but no genuine offer to those who are only external partakers of the covenant. Doing that goes outside the boundaries of Scripture, which is dangerous. God's promises are genuine and true. He is sincere in offering peace and pardon when His promises are sealed on our foreheads. In baptism, the faithfulness of God's promises is sealed to us. We may not curtail His grace, and yet, on the other hand, we must not deny the fact that those who will not repent and believe stand outside of salvation. Neither must we deny the fact that God is sovereign in all that He does. God fulfills His promises in a sovereign way.

The promise of salvation, which the Lord gave to Abraham, applied to Abraham's seed—to everyone who came forth from Abraham. Therefore they carry the name of "children of the covenant," or "children of the promise" (Acts 3:25). Yet, not all of Abraham's descendants are Abraham's children in truth. There are two kinds of branches, two kinds of children, two kinds of heirs and partakers of the covenant. Only those who do the works of Abraham are the spiritual seed of Abraham.

And what kind of work is this? It is believing in God, who justifies the ungodly. We read of Abraham, "Abraham believed God, and it was counted unto him for righteousness." Abraham considered God to be faithful. He entrusted his entire salvation to God. Likewise, Abraham's children are those who no longer trust in their own works or virtues, but who, as condemned sinners, trust in the righteousness of Christ. They are, according to Galatians 3, the true children of Abraham. The apostle says, "Know ye therefore that they which are of faith, the same are the children of Abraham" (v. 7).

We cannot be true children of Abraham without doing the works of Abraham. We must part with sin and seek that city which has foundations, whose Builder and Maker is God. Only then will we belong to the true church. The true church consists of pilgrims who live as guests and strangers here below. Just bearing the name of being Abraham's seed will not save us; John the Baptist said, "And think not to say within yourselves, We have Abraham to our father: for I say unto you, that God is able of these stones to raise up children unto Abraham" (Matt. 3:9). People who rely on outward baptism are like Israel at the time of Hophni and Phinehas; the ark had to go up in the battle with the army, but Israel did not need the God of the ark. They were defeated with the ark in their midst and, likewise, we will go lost eternally with our baptism. We need the God of baptism.

Our privileges should drive us out to repent and believe because, through these privileges, the kingdom of God has come close. It is as if salvation has been laid down at our feet, and therefore we hear the words of John the Baptist, "The kingdom of heaven is at hand: repent ye, and believe the gospel" (Mark 1:15). How important it is to constantly keep this in mind. On the one hand, the Lord must keep us from despising the privileges of those who are baptized; but, on the other hand, He must keep us from becoming people who say, "We are Abraham's children" without doing the works of Abraham.

We are, therefore, admonished by the privileges of baptism "to bring forth fruits worthy of faith and repentance." The holy sign of baptism urges us to seek God and His grace. We ought to live for the honor of God. The holy sign sets us apart from the world, but woe to us when we do not live a life separated from this ungodly world. Being born to Christian parents is such a great privilege. Our cradle could have been in the darkness of heathenism. But He caused us to be born within the bounds of His covenant. He brought us under the preaching of His gospel and God's grace is offered to us. Oh, do not consider these things to be of little value; it is not an insignificant thing to be baptized!

Great are the privileges, but more than privilege is required for salvation. We need the works of Abraham. We need Abraham's grace. Yes, we need Abraham's God. If only all of us would seek the God of our baptism and say with Augustine,

"Oh God, my heart does not find rest in me, until it finds rest in Thee."

We cannot escape the fact that baptism is either to life or to death. Baptism will either testify for us or against us, for no one can listen to the gospel without being held accountable. The gospel will be either a savor of life to life or a savor of death to death.

What will it be like to be baptized and then to die without having faith in Christ and stand before the throne of the Lamb! The wrath of the covenant will come on us because, with Esau, we have despised the blessings of the covenant. Then baptism will become a seal of our condemnation. This is what Paul emphasizes, "Of how much sorer punishment, suppose ye, shall he be thought worthy, who hath trodden under foot the Son of God, and hath counted the blood of the covenant, wherewith he was sanctified, an unholy thing?" (Heb. 10:29). Those words, "wherewith he was sanctified," make the punishment all the more severe. Having been separated from the world by baptism and yet to count the blood of Christ unclean, will mean to be judged by Him who called unto us many times, "Oh, that you would know, even today, the things which belong unto your peace!" It will mean to be cursed by Him who taught in our streets as He did in Capernaum. The wrath of the covenant will come on us if the offered blessing of the covenant will not bring us to repentance. Therefore, as the Holy Spirit says, "To day if ye will hear his voice, harden not your hearts, as in the provocation, in the day of temptation in the wilderness: when your fathers tempted me and proved me" (Heb. 3:7-9).

The Second Baptismal Question
Secondly, whether you acknowledge the doctrine which is contained in the Old and New Testament, and in the articles of the Christian faith, and which is taught here in this Christian church, to be the true and perfect doctrine of salvation?

We discussed the first question in detail, but we can be brief with the second question. The parents are asked whether they agree with the doctrine of the church. Why is this necessary? They have already confessed agreement when they made confession of faith, didn't they? Note, however, that at baptism the parents do not stand before the congregation simply as members, but as parents. They will be the ones who will educate and provide for the children to be baptized. They take on themselves the task of instructing, and thus the church wishes to know whether the children will be reared in the right doctrine.

The church feels responsible for the children because they are *her* children—the seed of the congregation. The baptized children must be raised up in accordance with the confession of the church to which they belong. They are born in her fold, and by baptism they become members of the church. So the church has a right to ask this question of the parents in order to know that the children will be instructed well. The church wants to be certain that the children are raised up in a Christian manner as much as is possible.

That is why the parents are asked this question. The parents will be instructors and pass on the knowledge of the Scriptures to the next generation. God gives to the parents the office of teacher. It can be compared with someone who takes upon himself a church office; he does this only after he has been told what his office means, and after he has answered the relevant questions. Likewise, the parents are told what their office means. Among other things, it means to instruct the children in the true doctrine. Therefore, the parents, as the providers for the child, make a confession of faith on behalf of the child with the hope that in the future, when the child grows up, he will take this confession for himself and do public confession of faith before the congregation.

The form speaks of "the doctrine which is contained in the Old and New Testament, and in the articles of the Christian faith." The confession of the parents concerns doctrine according to the Scriptures, as summarized in the twelve articles of faith—not the ideas of some important person or a synod, but doctrine that agrees with Scripture. The doctrine of truth is not a theological thesis of some theologian; it is the doctrine of the Scriptures. In contrast to Rome, whose councils are given a greater authority than the Scriptures, a Reformed Christian acknowledges that the Scriptures have the highest authority.

The question then continues: "and which is taught here in this Christian church." Now the question becomes a little more direct. The parents are asked whether they acknowledge that the doctrine of the Scriptures is the doctrine taught in the church where they are having their children baptized.

The word "here" has caused many disputes. In the days of early Remonstrantism (around 1600), many objected to this word. Those who did not wish to accept the Reformed doctrine refused to answer this question. Even before the year 1600, there were liberal ministers who considered the word "here" too restrictive and who brought their objection to the synod of Middelburg. The synod of Middelburg accommodated their objections and answered the question, "Which questions are to be used for the administration of baptism?" by saying they should stay with the accepted formula but were free to use or leave out the phrase "the doctrine which is taught here" (Question 21 of the Synod of Middelburg, 1581). This made it possible for parents who did not agree with the doctrine of the local church to answer affirmatively to the questions. It meant a victory for ministers with a remonstrant inclination.

In the Hague, another bitter dispute originated between Peter Plancius and Johannes Uitenbogaerdt concerning the same phrase. This dispute particularly arose after the baptism of a grandchild of Uitenbogaerdt in a service where Plancius officiated. The orthodox people demanded the words "which is taught here" to be read. The defenders of the doctrine of the Reformation demanded that the parents would agree with the doctrine of Scriptures, but also with the doctrine of the local church. Since the Remonstrants did not want this they essentially announced that they did not believe the doctrine of the local church to be the doctrine of the Scriptures.

The synod of Dordrecht of 1618-1619 discussed this differ-

ence, but nothing can be found about it in the minutes. Revisionists were appointed who drafted a report, but no other
information is available. Yet Jacobus Trigland, who was a member of the Synod, writes about it, saying, "The addition of the
word 'here' or the words 'in this church' has been approved by
the national Synod of Dordrecht in 1619, being in agreement
with a prior decision made in 1613 by the ministers of Amster-
dam." This proves that the issue was discussed and that the
Synod rejected the remonstrant opinion, adhering to the original version. (The original version of Datheen reads, "Whether
you acknowledge the doctrine taught *here* and which is contained in the Old and New Testament, and in the articles of the
Christian faith"). Festus Hommius, the revisionist appointed by
the Synod, says in an appendix of the revised report: "The form
for the administration of baptism has been restored by the
National Synod." Thus, even though the minutes are silent
about it, the Synod did confront the issue. This is sufficient support for us to keep to the version approved by the Synod of
Dordrecht, and thus to read the words "which is taught here in
this Christian church."

Nevertheless, I acknowledge that these words can cause
problems for conscientious parents. During the time of the
Secession,[3] many parents could not answer this question
because they felt that the doctrine was not pure in their local
church. Many traveled to Rev. Hendrik de Cock in Ulrum to
have their children baptized. This resulted in conflicts between
these parents and their local church sessions. In contrast to
many parents, who had no problem in having their children baptized in churches where the doctrine of the Reformation was
rejected, these parents knew the significance of the issues. The
doctrine of the Scriptures ought to be the doctrine of the local
church. What is not according to the Word will not stand. We

---

[3] "Secession" refers to the separation by various congregations from the Dutch
State church, which occurred in 1834. The main reason for this split was liberal theological preaching in the State church; people were taught that living a
decent and good life was sufficient to meet God.

must raise our children with true doctrine, and that is what parents agree to when they answer the question.

I hope we all realize more and more what it means, and before whom we answer, when we say "Yes" to this question. It should drive us to God, because we need Him. He who lacks wisdom may, according to God's own Word, ask it from Him, who gives liberally and upbraids not. My wish and desire is that this may be the result of this second baptismal question.

The Third Baptismal Question

Thirdly. Whether you promise and intend to see these children, when come to the years of discretion (whereof you are either parent or witness), instructed and brought up in the aforesaid doctrine, or help or cause them to be instructed therein, to the utmost of your power.

The words "whereof you are either parent[4] or witness" are not found in the original version of the form. However, it has been the custom to use these words since the Synod of Dordrecht, held in 1574. At that time, it was customary to baptize very soon after birth. In fact, baptism was administered so quickly that the mother had often not recovered sufficiently to be present. Therefore, the father presented the child for baptism, which is why the mother is not mentioned. This has changed. We now wait until the mother has regained her strength and can be present at the baptismal service. However, we should not wait for an unnecessarily long period of time before we have our children baptized; they should be baptized as soon as is practical.

Further, the question mentions a "witness." If the parents could not be present when their child was baptized, due to sickness or any other circumstance, then witnesses were permitted. If the church could not accept the parents to answer the questions, for just reasons, the witnesses could even present the children for baptism. However, this is not right. Witnesses ought never to replace the parents. They do not have civil authority over the

---

[4] The Dutch version reads "father" instead of "parent" and the following comments should be read in this context.

child, unless they are guardians. If the parents are still alive and their child has not been taken out of their care, the church should realize that the parents are the lawful representatives of the child. In this case, the witnesses generally cannot pledge anything to the church regarding the upbringing of the child.

The custom of having witnesses present at baptism has a historical background. Scripture does not speak of witnesses; it is based on a custom traced back to the first Christians. When an adult Gentile wanted to become a Christian and be baptized, he was brought to a bishop by a witness. This witness testified to the bishop of the sincere desire of the person to become a Christian. He testified that the person had an honest profession and that he lived a Christian life. Furthermore, the witness had to ensure that the person to be baptized would be instructed in the true doctrine.

This system of using a witness changed when, in accordance with God's demand and the content of God's covenant, infant baptism increasingly became the predominant form of baptism. The parents now act as witnesses at baptism. Augustine said that the parents should be witnesses for their children, the masters should be witnesses for the children of their slaves, and dedicated virgins should be witnesses for abandoned children. Later, it was the custom that a stranger brought the child to baptism rather than the parents. These strangers were members of the church and were called a "godfather" and "godmother." The godparents presented the child for baptism and also answered the questions, acting as spiritual parents of the child. Having separate godparents and true parents was intended to depict how much the spiritual upbringing differed from the carnal upbringing. It was an honor to have godparents, and particularly so when any prominent persons wanted to be the godparents. But making such a strong distinction between nature and grace is a Roman Catholic error; therefore, the Reformed Church restored to parents their original task of answering the questions.

Calvin emphasizes that baptism and the promises of baptism concerned the parents. In the church order of Geneva, the father was required to present the child for baptism and answer the questions. Calvin allowed witnesses to take over this task only in the absence of parents. The authors of the form for the administration of baptism thought likewise and therefore only mentioned the father. However, the custom of the people was stronger than the voice of the Reformation. Many synods dealt with this issue, and again and again they pointed out that witnesses were not required at baptism, although they left it to the discretion of the congregations whether or not witnesses could be present, because Scripture nowhere says anything against having multiple people care for the spiritual well-being of a child.

The issue was also discussed at the Synod of Dordrecht. It was pointed out that having witnesses present at a baptism was a custom that was discretionary. However, the Synod did say, "It is proper that such witnesses be taken who agree with the pure doctrine and are pious in their conversation" (Church Order, Article 57). Furthermore, in the same article, the synod insisted that the father would answer the questions and present the child for baptism. This article states: "The ministers shall do their best and put forth every effort to have the father present his child for baptism."

The synod desired to counteract the Roman Catholic influence of using witnesses at baptism. Rome teaches that the parents are the carnal procreators of the child, who have defiled the child with inherited sin. Therefore, through baptism, the church takes the child into her holy fold and the child is washed from its sin. But this must occur through spiritual parents—that is, the godparents. The Reformers opposed this doctrine and custom and restored the right of the parents to present their child for baptism. They understood that God's covenant continues from generation to generation. God made His covenant with Abraham and his seed, and propagates His Name from child to child and from generation to generation. The Lord uses the natural line of descent to confirm His covenant. How then could the faithfulness of this covenant be better depicted than when the parents present the child for baptism to receive the sign of the covenant? Therefore, the synods of Dordrecht (1574 and 1578, Article 61), Middelburg (1581, Article 40) and The Hague (1586, Article 61) strongly recommended that the ministers would ensure that the father present the child for baptism and that the role of the father not be inferior to that of the godparents. Like the Synod of Dordrecht of 1618-1619, the other synods decided that ministers should do their best to have the father present his child for baptism. They also expressly stated that witnesses had to stand next to the parents and only had to help instruct the children in their upbringing. They would have preferred to abandon the entire custom, but, because it was so entrenched in church life, they did not want to do it in a revolutionary manner.

Jacobus Koelman strongly objected to the custom. In his *The Duties of Parents*, he admonished parents to publicly give their promise to instruct their children in the truth and in godliness themselves. They should not take godfathers and godmothers since this was a human custom originating from the Roman Catholic Church, from which God's blessing could not be expected. Koelman and others were fighting against the custom of parents choosing rich and important people as godparents for the status and the gifts, while godliness and virtue were not even considered. Fortunately, this custom has disappeared. In very special circumstances—when the parents cannot do so—witnesses may present the children for baptism. But the witnesses may never replace the parents in their duties and responsibilities.

If we are consistent in applying the opinion of the Reformers, then the last question should be asked like this: "Thirdly. Whether you promise and intend to see this child (or these children), when come to the years of discretion (whereof you are the father), instructed and brought up in the aforesaid doctrine, or cause them to be instructed therein, to the utmost of your power." The words concerning the witnesses and "to help instruct" would then be left out.

Additionally, we should insist that the father presents the child for baptism and answers the questions. This also agrees with the biblical viewpoint concerning the presentation of a child for baptism. According to Scripture, the man is the head of the woman as Christ is the Head of the church, so it appears to be contrary to Scripture when the mother has the prominent role at baptism. Of course, this is only outward form, but with the administration of baptism in particular, which is the visible gospel, the visual aspect has an important function.

The aspects concerning witnesses can be left out without any problem or chance of offending or troubling the church. We should, therefore, do away with witnesses because it alludes to Rome. We must distance ourselves from this practice as far as we can, particularly in the ceremony of the administration of baptism. We should also first ask the father to answer the questions and then the mother. Further, we should not postpone the administration of baptism unnecessarily. But above all, we should pray that our hearts would be like the heart of Hannah, the mother of Samuel. She presented her child to the God of the covenant. Let us present our children in the same manner and dedicate our children to Him through upbringing and prayer.

There is something else in this question that deserves our attention—namely, the words "intend to." In our days, these words do not necessarily have the connotation of making a promise. However, the original wording in the sixteenth century meant to seriously resolve to do something or solemnly take responsibility for something. This meaning is lost somewhat in the current wording of the form. Considering that these words concern a promise made before God's holy countenance, it would be better if the form read, "Whether you promise and resolve to see," as it is more than an intention. It is an oath.

We should further note that the question says, "to see

instructed or help or cause them to be instructed to the utmost of your power." Parents must do everything in their power to instruct their child in the true doctrine, or cause their child to be instructed therein. This means they must utilize their talents to the utmost. They may not neglect this duty by making the argument, "We do not have enough knowledge to do this." It is the principle task of the parents to instruct their children. This means that they must send their children to a good Christian school and that they ensure their faithful attendance at the catechism classes. They must be willing to sacrifice something for this, because, one day, they will have to give an account of all these things.

There are many parents who do not do this. They never speak with their children about God and His service. Some catechism classes are poorly attended. Some parents never check whether their children study the questions and they never discuss the subject matter of the lessons with their children. If we live like this, then we do not instruct our children to the utmost of our power. On the other hand, this form addresses parents who are concerned with the salvation of their children. They do everything possible and yet they feel their shortcomings. Sincere parents know this by experience—how often our prayers for the conversion of our children are lukewarm. How often our instruction lacks love and serious-mindedness. How often is the attendance of catechism, school, and church just a custom. Yet, if with a praying heart we do all that we can, then the promise of the Lord will comfort us: He will pour His Spirit on our children (Isa. 44:3). We are not capable of converting our children; that is the work of God. Where our power comes short, we will need God's power. This is what comforted Job when he said, "I know that thou canst do everything." Our weakness brings us to God's power.

These three questions are answered with a single and solemn "Yes." The affirmative answer to these three questions is given in the presence of the Lord and before His holy congregation. On the great day, the parents will have to give an account of this "Yes" because the questions and answer at the administration of baptism concern matters of eternity. This makes the answer serious and solemn. Therefore, we may well cry out, "O let Thy Spirit be my constant aid!"

An oath is taken before the all-seeing Lord. Oh, that we would feel the solemnity and weight of this oath! It would make us to instruct our children "to the utmost of our power" and call upon God's power to make our children true children of Abraham, bringing forth the works of Abraham.

CHAPTER 5

The Administration of Baptism

Then the Minister of God's Word, in baptizing, shall say, N., I baptize thee in the name of the Father, and of the Son, and of the Holy Ghost. Amen.

It is customary in Reformed churches for the minister to speak a few words to the parents after they have answered the questions. This is called the baptismal address. It is difficult to prove historically that the Reformers intended to have such an address take place; on the contrary, we must honestly acknowledge that the authors have not allowed a place for this in the form for the administration of baptism. In the Paltz, it was not unusual that after the "Yes" of the parents, the minister admonished the parents. However, Datheen did not adopt this custom. That is why the idea of a personal address is not included in our form.

Actually, the synods insisted on reading the form as written—that is, without giving a free address. The Synod of Dordrecht of 1574 stipulated in article 66, "And, because it is dangerous that the ministers themselves give a special admonishment prior to the administration of baptism, it has been decided that the formula, of which a summary has been sent to the ministers, would be the same." This summary refers to the abstract of the form for the administration of baptism, which was sent to the ministers for their use.

The Synod did say in article 63 that the ministers must bind the parents to the instruction of their children and to admonish the witnesses present. However, this must be understood correctly. The ministers "bind" the parents by asking them to answer "Yes." Furthermore, the admonition was directed to the witnesses who attended the baptismal service. It was not to be done by means of a free address, but by a formula which the Synod of 1574 adopted from the Paltz and which was appended to the form. The wording of this admonishment was as follows: "Afterwards, the minister will speak thus: Furthermore, as each Christian is duty bound by love to admonish his neighbor, both young and old, to godliness, I will likewise pray and admonish particularly you, who stand here as witnesses of the baptism of this child, that, when this child grows up, you will help direct him or her in the ways of the Lord, so that this child may rightly experience his or her baptism." However, the editors of the Synod of Dordrecht of 1618-1619 deleted this section. In this flourishing period, the church was satisfied with the form alone and baptismal addresses were not given.

The introduction of the addresses can be traced back to the decline of the church. In the time of the Secession, orthodox ministers felt the need to point out in a short address to the parents and congregation what baptism really means. The reason for doing this was that the churches had backslidden so much from Reformed truth. This is most likely why the custom of the baptismal speech was introduced in churches, particularly in the congregations that belonged to the Secession.

Such an address may enliven the baptismal ceremony and be used to make the parents understand the solemnity of baptism. Therefore, there is no reason to do away with this custom provided the address is secondary to the form. It must be nothing more than an explanation of baptism. The Synod of 1574 thought it to be "dangerous," and it can be, when we proclaim our own opinions about baptism. The minister has to keep to the doctrine as explained in the form for the administration of baptism, and he must especially let the Word of God speak. Thus, the baptismal address is not necessary, but may be edifying, provided the minister adheres to the doctrine of the Reformed confession.

After this, the time for the administration of baptism has come. The element that has to be used to administer baptism is pure water. There is no difference between sprinkling or immersion. Immersion does more clearly depict the meaning of baptism, but for practical reasons the Western church uses sprinkling. The volume of water is not the most important matter in the administration of baptism.

The place where baptism must be administered is in the midst of the congregation. Baptism is a visible gospel; it must be able to be seen by the congregation.

The Baptismal Formula

At the administration of baptism, the minister speaks thus: "I baptize thee in the Name of the Father, and of the Son, and of the Holy Ghost." Usually, the minister will sprinkle with water three times while he says the baptismal formula. Our forefathers did not like this habit; they preferred to sprinkle only once. The Synod of 1574 decided in article 65, "The brethren feel that it is preferred and best, if the churches used a single sprinkling when administering baptism. However they have decided to condone the habit of sprinkling three times in those churches where it is the current custom, until such time that the other manner can be introduced." Sprinkling three times was a custom used in the Roman Catholic Church. Our forefathers desired instead to point to the unity between the Father, the Son, and the Holy Ghost and, therefore, they preferred to sprinkle only once.

The most important matter of the ceremony is this phrase: "In the Name of the Father, and of the Son, and of the Holy Ghost." The apostles baptized in the name of Jesus. When this is said in the Acts of the Apostles, it pointed to the doctrine of Jesus. (Likewise, we read in 1 Cor. 10:2 of being baptized to Moses.) This does not mean, therefore, that they did not baptize in the name of the triune God; we know from very early sources that the Christian church did. Justin, the martyr who died in the year 165 A.D., mentions the same formula as the one we use.

The reason why the apostles did not immediately follow Christ's command to baptize in the Name of the Father, and of the Son, and of the Holy Ghost is given by Calvin when he says, "They did this because all the gifts of God presented in baptism are found in Christ alone."

In baptism, the triune God seals solemnly His covenant and His promises. He swears with an oath, "Jehovah's truth will stand forever, His covenant-bonds He will not sever." The reason why the Name of the triune God has to be mentioned when baptism is administered is explained by Calvin in his commentary on Matthew 28:19: "There are good reasons why the Father, the Son, and the Holy Spirit, are expressly mentioned; for there is no other way in which the efficacy of baptism can be experienced than when we begin with the unmerited mercy of the Father, who reconciles us to Himself by the only begotten Son; next, Christ comes forward with the sacrifice of His death; and at length, the Holy Spirit is likewise added, by whom He washes and regenerates us, and, in short, makes us partakers of His benefits." Three Persons show their saving work in baptism and each of them seals that they will work what is necessary for salvation. Faith may cry out, "This God is our God. He will lead us, even unto death."

The form says, "In the Name." The Greek word has the connotation of "in communion with the Name of the triune God." Thus, it does not only mean that baptism is commanded by God, but it also designates a transfer into the communion with the triune God. Thus, "in the Name" says what God wants for His church: He wants to bring them into communion with Himself and to be a God of full salvation to them. His name stands for His essence and being.

Baptism seals to the believer that "we have an eternal covenant with God." The words, "In the Name of the Father, and of the Son, and of the Holy Ghost" mean to be brought into a different communion. They mean to be brought from being

under the power of sin, the world, and Satan into the communion with the Father, the Son, and the Holy Spirit. This is the
essence of being baptized: we no longer belong to the world, but
to the kingdom of God (1 Pet. 2:9). The baptized child must be
brought from the kingdom of Satan into the kingdom of God,
to be in communion with God.

But at the same time, the administration of baptism in the
name of the triune God is a divine sealing of His covenant and
promise. It is just like someone who writes his name under an
important document as a sign that he guarantees its content.
The triune God puts His Name under His Word and promise,
guaranteeing that everything He spoke in His Word is true. So
this sacrament is a seal of God's promises. The eternal
covenant stands unmovable. God's people are comforted that
they have an eternal covenant of grace with God and may say
in faith, "Yet he hath made with me an everlasting covenant"
(2 Sam. 23:5).

But the visible church may also be comforted here. In the
administration of baptism, God promises to establish His
covenant among her and her seed, and to gather His elect
church from her. And He confirms all this by underwriting it
with His triune name. The sinner may take comfort here,
because God fixes a seal to His Word. He swears that it is certain and true that Jesus Christ has come into the world to save
sinners. Should we then not pray, "Do, Lord, as Thou hast spoken"? God not only seals His covenant promises but also all
what He has promised in the gospel. What will it be on the last
day to have not believed this message? It will mean that we have
called God a liar, for "He that believeth not God hath made him
a liar; because he believeth not the record that God gave of his
Son" (1 John 5:10).

To conclude, I will say something about the stanza of the
song sung at the administration of baptism. The singing is not
mentioned in the form and, therefore, is not necessary. Again,
it has simply become a custom. Following the spirit of the
Synod of Dordrecht concerning minor issues, I would say that

it may be done. However, when the congregation does sing, it should be a stanza that concerns the covenant of God. Psalter 425:5 is very suitable. It is difficult to change customs; I only point out how it was originally intended and what would be the best thing to do.

◆

CHAPTER 6

The Prayer of Thanksgiving

Almighty God and merciful Father, we thank and praise thee, that thou hast forgiven us, and our children, all our sins, through the blood of thy beloved Son Jesus Christ, and received us through thy Holy Spirit as members of thine only begotten Son, and adopted us to be thy children, and sealed and confirmed the same unto us by holy baptism; we beseech thee, through the same Son of thy love, that thou wilt be pleased always to govern these baptized children by thy Holy Spirit, that they may be piously and religiously educated, increase and grow up in the Lord Jesus Christ, that they then may acknowledge thy fatherly goodness and mercy, which thou hast shown to them and us, and live in all righteousness, under our only Teacher, King, and High Priest, Jesus Christ; and manfully fight against, and overcome sin, the devil and his whole dominion, to the end that they may eternally praise and magnify thee, and thy Son Jesus Christ, together with the Holy Ghost, the one only true God. Amen.

This prayer of thanksgiving has often been misunderstood. Many ministers did not even want to use it and read the form only up to the prayer of thanksgiving. Others, such as Abraham Kuyper, Jr., took it to mean that our Reformed fathers viewed all children of the visible church as regenerated. I shall try to explain the prayer of thanksgiving so that we understand the real meaning.

First, we must understand that it is the congregation praying here. The congregation begins the prayer of thanksgiving with

"Almighty God and merciful Father." After the administration of baptism, the congregation thinks of the omnipotence and mercy of God. This should not surprise us; the elect church of Jesus Christ owes her salvation to the power and mercy of God. Furthermore, they call God "Father." The fatherly love of God toward His church is shown in the sacraments, and baptism may be called a pledge of God's genuine love and faithfulness toward His people. As a Father, who is concerned about the comfort and salvation of His children, God has instituted the sacraments for the strengthening of their faith. Yes, in baptism God extends His fatherly love even unto the children of the faithful.

"We thank and praise thee." The congregation gives thanks to God. Three things are necessary to know in order to live and to die happily; thankfulness is one of these. Many church-going people do nothing but thank and praise God. They have nothing left to ask because they have not learned their misery. But there is also a different kind of church attendee, who does not forget the first part—the misery. But they can so easily forget that third part—thankfulness. Then the scales tip the other way and we never hear thanksgiving and praise. The prayer of thanksgiving here wants to teach the congregation to give thanks to the God of the covenant for His benefits. She praises God, exalting His honor—the honor of His sovereign goodness and covenantal faithfulness.

We should realize how much reason we have for thanksgiving. We must read the prayer of thanksgiving in the context of the whole form. The form begins with the message and confession that we, with our children, have been conceived and born in sin, and therefore are children of wrath. Then the forms speaks of the wonder of grace—that God establishes a covenant with us and our children, and that He gives His promises to us and our children. God has sealed this covenant and these promises in the baptism of the children. Why, then, would the congregation not have a desire to give thanks to God for all this?

Baptism has been administered and the promises have been sealed. Now the congregation desires to give thanks to God. In this prayer of thanksgiving, the church follows in the footsteps of her father, Abraham. After the institution of circumcision and after having heard the faithfulness of God's covenant, we read that "Abraham fell upon his face, and laughed" (Gen. 17:17). Abraham laughed because he marveled at the promises of God to him and his seed. The Dutch annotations say concerning Abraham's laughing: "Not because of doubting, like Sarah, but because of wonder and gladness."

Why does the congregation give thanks to God? The form says that "thou hast forgiven us, and our children, all our sins, through the blood of thy beloved Son Jesus Christ, and received us through thy Holy Spirit as members of thine only begotten Son, and adopted us to be thy children, and sealed and confirmed the same unto us by holy baptism."

These words, in particular, have met strong objections because they were incorrectly interpreted in a subjective manner, as if they say that each baptized child has received the forgiveness of sins and become a partaker of regeneration. This sounds like presupposed regeneration. Therefore, some wanted it read "the elect children," or they wished to leave it out altogether. However, to change the form is to change the Reformed doctrine. The form, the prayer of thanksgiving included, must be read as written. We may not change this arbitrarily.

The prayer concerns "these baptized children." How can it be that, after the administration of baptism, thanks is given to God because He has forgiven us and our children all our sins and has adopted us for His children? We know from experience that this is not the case for many baptized children, don't we? If we reason like this, we err, because our reasoning pertains to the baptized child, whereas the authors' reasoning pertains to the promise God has made in baptism. To understand these words, we must remember what baptism seals and confirms—namely, God's covenant and promises. When we discussed the significance of baptism, we saw how the Lord promises to the visible church that He will keep His covenant with her. The Lord promises to work in the midst of the visible church with the grace of

His covenant, as He promised to do through circumcision to the visible church of the Israelites. Thus, God promises that He will gather His elect from among her and will propagate His Name from generation to generation.

All the promises of the covenant of grace are sealed and confirmed by baptism and, afterward, the congregation gives thanks to God. If we read the prayer properly, we see that the church does not give thanks for something that is yet to come, but for something she knows she already possesses. We do not say "shall forgive" or "shall receive" but "hast forgiven and received." How is it possible to say this? How could the Reformers at the Synod of Dordrecht approve such a prayer? Many people who carefully read the first part of the prayer of thanksgiving ask these questions. Without a doubt, there seems to be a great difficulty in these words. Yet, I think that the difficulty lies with us and not with the form. We must not think of it as received grace or something like that. All emphasis must be on what God seals and confirms in baptism—namely, His promise that "I will be thy God and the God of thy seed." The congregation gives thanks to God for what He has promised. We do not say, "We'll wait and see whether God will fulfill His promise." No, the congregation desires to thank God, believing that His promises are faithful. When someone who is totally trustworthy promises you something, what should you do when you receive his promise? You should humbly thank him. We must see the prayer of thanksgiving here in that light. God has sealed His promises in baptism, and the congregation has no reason to distrust such a God. Therefore we give thanks to Him for what He has promised. Only if we through faith understand the meaning of the administration of baptism, can we thank God in this manner. We must see that God seals His covenant promises in baptism.

Parents who receive comfort from the sacrament of baptism can understand this. From their hearts they join in the prayer and say, "Almighty God and merciful Father, we thank and praise thee, that thou hast forgiven us, and our children, all our sins, through the blood of thy beloved Son Jesus Christ, and received us through thy Holy Spirit as members of thine only begotten Son, and adopted us to be thy children." Faith is speaking in this prayer. Unbelief questions God, saying, "God may say all this, but is it really true?" But faith cleaves to God's faithfulness and knows it will possess everything in the promise. The true church knows that they deal with a God who is "yea and amen." Abraham had such faith. After having received the promise of God, he fell with his face on the ground, thanked God, and did not doubt God's promise.

That these were the beliefs of the Reformers is evident from their writings. Again and again, you will find a tender gratitude for what God promised to be for them and their children in baptism. Note also, that it is exactly the *promise* of God in baptism for which thanks is given. Thanks is given for the washing away of sins and the work of the Holy Spirit, which is exactly that what the Heidelberg Catechism says is the promise of baptism. Question 74 asks: "Are infants also to be baptized?" The answer is, "Yes, for since they, as well as the adult, are included in the covenant and church of God; and since redemption from sin by the blood of Christ, and the Holy Ghost, the author of faith, is promised to them no less than to the adult." The congregation gives thanks to the covenant God for this promise. There is no reason to doubt His promises, and therefore she says "has received." She leaves the fulfillment of this promise to the sovereignty of God.

I know that for many there is a great and sometimes insurmountable difficulty in this prayer of thankfulness. But if we make the effort to understand the language of our Reformed fathers, we will gain a clearer perspective on this. They do not say that the parents and children of the congregation already are partakers of the forgiveness of sins. The words "hast forgiven us and our children," which are often misunderstood, mean the promise of forgiveness in the preaching of the gospel. In the gospel, and particularly in the visible gospel of baptism, God offers the forgiveness of sins in Christ to us and to our children.

Comrie says, "We understand the granting, proffering, and giving to mean that the things which are thus proffered unto us are truly granted and given unto us from God in the promise of the gospel, and understand these words, although they sound different from one another, to mean the one and the same thing" (*Heidelberg Catechism*, p. 450). The grace of the forgiveness of sins and the adoption of children is granted in the offer of the gospel. To become a possessor of this grace, the child must be converted and believe, but in the promise of the gospel, God offers the forgiveness of sin.

So, in the first place, we have seen that the congregation humbly gives thanks to the Lord for the promise sealed in baptism. In the second place, we noted the language used to thank God for granting His promises of the gospel. Now there is a third reason why the congregation gives thanks to God.

Before the child was baptized, the congregation prayed for forgiveness of sins through the blood of Christ, and for the adoption of our children through the Holy Spirit. Now, following this prayer, we have the prayer of thanksgiving. To get a better understanding of this prayer, I would therefore like to quote Fruytier, a man highly esteemed by Comrie. Fruytier said the following:

> Here, we should carefully note who it is that gives thanks. Surely, this giving of thanks is done in the name of all true believers, who only are the true members of Christ and His church. These, having the Spirit who shows them what they have been given by God, can in this manner give thanks for themselves and their children unto God who in time will fulfill the promise: I will be a God unto you and your seed. When they now pray for the children, who have been legally admitted to baptism, they trust that, for as long as the opposite does not become evident, God has heard their prayers. Therefore, they give thanks for the same children, for which they prayed God that He would incorporate them into His Son. They thank God for answering their prayer and speak of the children as children who have been incorporated already upon the prayer of the whole congregation. Not only does the

prayer of a Christian avail much, but, according to the instruction of John (1 John 5:14), this is the confidence of a Christian, which he has with God, that if we pray for something according to His will, He will hear us. Now, all Christians, who have been taught by God, know that when a Christian asks something of God, this is done with subjection to God's sovereignty. Whereas God, on the one hand, has openly proclaimed that He will have mercy on whom He will have mercy, and that there are but few chosen among those who are called, on the other hand says, "I will be your God and the God of your seed," so they pray according to God's will when, acknowledging these things also, they pray for the children which are baptized, and therefore go so far in praying as the promises of God do. Because God does not reveal His will in this, and does not exclude the children who are baptized, they humbly and believingly trust that God has heard them and therefore after their prayer will view these children as if God had looked upon them in mercy, although always acknowledging God's sovereignty and the death-worthiness of the baptized children (*The Great Privilege of Children of Christians*, pp. 150-151).

Those who carefully read Fruytier's explanation will observe that our fathers did not consider the prayers, which are part of the form, to be superfluous. We often see so little value in the form prayer offered by the entire congregation, but our fathers did see the value of it. Their thoughts concerning the death of young children were founded on their belief that we should not think too little of God's mercy and the form prayer offered before the administration of baptism ("Minutes of the Synod of Dordrecht 1618-1619," p. 619).

Following the giving of thanks, there is a prayerful plea. The congregation is asked to pray, "We beseech thee, through the same Son of thy love, that thou wilt be pleased always to govern these baptized children by thy Holy Spirit." Thanksgiving has changed into requests. The congregation cannot refrain from praying for her children. She is concerned about her children with high-priestly pity. What she desires from God now con-

cerns the life of the child in particular. She asks that the child
may receive the fulfillment of the promises. God's promises
must be worked out in the way of conversion and faith, and that
is why the congregation prays. The emphasis in the prayer is on
whether God will govern the child through His Holy Spirit. The
parents have made the promise that the child would be governed
in a Christian and godly manner, but, in the prayer of thanksgiving, the congregation looks past the parents and all that is
human and lays the child at the feet of God, asking Him to govern him or her through His Holy Spirit. She wants God to be
King in the life of this young child. Only when Satan is cast
from the throne of the heart and God ascends it, to govern the
child through His Spirit, will it be well with the child. The greatest misery of a fallen sinner is that he wants to be his own king.
He thinks that it will give him the greatest happiness if he were
master and lord of himself, but instead it gives him the greatest,
eternal misery. True happiness is when God is his King and
when he serves and fears God as such. True freedom and salvation for man lies in the bond with God. The congregation
supplicates for this bond with God for her children when she
prays, "Oh Lord, govern this child through Thy Holy Spirit."

When that happens, then the following will be true also:
"that they may be piously and religiously educated, increase and
grow up in the Lord Jesus Christ, that they then may acknowledge thy fatherly goodness and mercy, which thou hast shown
to them and us." When God governs the child with His Holy
Spirit, their upbringing will bear fruit. Without the work of the
Spirit, even the best upbringing will have no results. History
teaches us that godly parents sometimes bring forth ungodly
children. But when God's Spirit governs the child, he subjects
himself willingly to the Christian education given by his parents,
and he is truly raised to live a Christian and godly life. Only then
will he increase and grow up in the Lord Jesus, and increase in
stature, strength, understanding, and personality. However, the
congregation also desires an increasing and maturing in the
Lord Jesus Christ. Most parents anxiously wonder, "How will

this child turn out when he or she grows up?" The congregation asks the same question: many children have been baptized in her midst; how will they grow up? She casts her fears and worries before the covenant God and prays that He will make them increase and grow up in the Lord Jesus Christ.

"That they then may acknowledge thy fatherly goodness and mercy, which thou hast shown to them and us." In baptism, the Lord has shown fatherly goodness and mercy. Calvin called baptism a proof of God's mercy toward us. God had pity on the child and allowed the child to be born to Christian parents, separated the child from the world, and brought the child to the holy courts of His covenant. The child came into this world as a child of wrath, but God says to this child, "As I live, saith the Lord God, I have no pleasure in the death of the wicked; but that the wicked turn from his way and live" (Ezek. 33:11). He spoke to the child even before the child itself could speak.

This fatherly goodness has been shown to the whole congregation. Therefore, the prayer of the congregation is that the child may *know* this. Many who are baptized do not know this privilege and despise it. The prayer of the congregation is that this child, or these children, will not walk that way. The congregation asks the covenant God to circumcise the heart. The Old Testament church could circumcise the flesh, the New Testament church can cleanse with water, but only God can circumcise the heart and cleanse the soul with the blood of Jesus Christ.

The congregation must realize that as far as the upbringing of the children is concerned, they are dependent on the work of the Holy Spirit. The law of God's kingdom is always this: "Not by might, nor by power, but by my spirit, saith the Lord of hosts" (Zech. 4:6).

The authors teach the church to ask God to make the children deny their natural inclinations and receive a new desire through His Spirit to acknowledge God's fatherly goodness. Despite their privileges, the natural inclination of all children, baptized children included, is to despise God's privileges as Esau did. The congregation fears for such a despising of the privileges and prays, "That they then may acknowledge thy fatherly goodness and mercy, which thou hast shown to them and us."

Young people, do not take this privilege for granted, but acknowledge that it comes from God, who gave you your Christian family. Sometimes we look at children of worldly families and we say that we are never allowed any fun; we wished we were born in a family where everything is allowed! But what is the real case? We read of the ungodly and their children (Psalter 135:4):

> *They that trust in treasured gold,*
> *Though they boast of wealth untold,*
> *None can bid his brother live,*
> *None to God a ransom give.*

This is reality! They belong to the great majority of the world whom God allows to walk according to the thoughts of their own hearts, unless grace intervenes. However, God still desires to deal with you. He already spoke to you when you could neither think nor speak, and He had you baptized in His holy name. It is not insignificant to be born under and to live in a covenant relationship with God—that is, to live under the proclamation of the gospel and to hear God proffering peace and pardon. A choice is required of you. You either accept or reject God's covenant; you either follow in the footsteps of Esau and despise God's covenant, or follow in the footsteps of Jacob and wrestle to obtain the blessing of the covenant. It is either one or the other. The former shall lead to a heavier condemnation than your unbaptized friends, but the latter will lead to a seat with Abraham, Isaac, and Jacob in the kingdom of God. Having been separated from the majority of the world and brought within the courts of God's covenant carries such a great responsibility! The gospel is a savor of life unto life or a savor of death unto death. Oh, learn to *know* your privilege, so that you learn to wrestle with the covenant God like Jacob did. Then it can be said of you what is written concerning Jacob, "He wept, and made supplication unto him" (Hosea 12:4).

"And live in all righteousness, under our only Teacher, King and High Priest, Jesus Christ; and manfully fight against, and overcome sin, the devil and his whole dominion." The life of a Christian is impossible without Christ. Therefore, the bond with Christ is the subject of the prayer of the congregation. The congregation prays to God that the baptized children may have Christ as their Teacher, King, and High Priest. And the baptized children of the congregation will have to learn to fight—that is the main content of this petition. Only a few moments ago, the child received the mark of Christ. This corresponds beautifully with the Roman military oath, which was called a sacrament also. The child received the sacrament; it is as if a military oath has been given. Now, growing up, the child must keep this oath to fight against sin, the devil, and his whole dominion. A holy war should be fought, as Bunyan described it. Yet this can never be done in our own strength. That is why the congregation asks for the power of and communion with the Lord Jesus Christ as Teacher, King, and High Priest.

Christ must become our Teacher, and we must consider it to be our greatest honor to be His pupils. That means that we learn to know our foolishness. Otherwise, we will despise His lessons. Those who have learned their foolishness will cleave to Him as a Teacher, like the apostle who said, "Thou hast the words of eternal life."

To be under Christ as King means that we no longer rule ourselves. It means that we are unable to do anything in our own strength, but it also means to call out with Jehoshaphat, "For we have no might against this great company that cometh against us; neither know we what to do: but our eyes are upon thee" (2 Chr. 20:12).

To be under Christ as High Priest means to be unable to approach God alone. That is why Israel needed a priest. We will not learn to need a Priest such as Christ until we learn that we can never come before God by ourselves. But "let us therefore come boldly unto the throne of grace" (Heb. 4:16).

In this manner, the child will have to learn to fight and to seek his or her entire salvation and strength in Christ Jesus. This is what the congregation prays. She desires that her children may live the life of a true Christian under Jesus as Teacher, King, and High Priest. Essentially, she asks for a restoration of the office of fallen man—a restoration of the image of God.

"To the end that they may eternally praise and magnify thee, and thy Son Jesus Christ, together with the Holy Ghost, the one only true God. Amen." This is why the congregation prays for all these blessings: she has the honor of the triune covenant God in mind. The child was baptized in the Name of the Father, and of the Son, and of the Holy Spirit, and now the congregation has as her strongest desire that the Name of the Father, the Son, and the Holy Spirit may be eternally praised and magnified. This is the ultimate goal of the prayer of the congregation.

Having considered the prayers of the church in this manner, we can understand the Reformers of the Synod of Dordrecht when they said of young children who passed away, "That one would not esteem the prayers of the church lightly."

Where the honor of God is intended, God gives fallen man His salvation. A true parent will plead with the covenant God to turn away that terrible calamity of going lost forever from their children. Parents' hearts will cry out, "Have mercy on me and my children, O Lord, Thou Son of David."

Yet, there is a higher and deeper motive for pleading for the salvation of the children, and that is the thought that their children would be instruments that curse God. This thought hurts the heart the most. Faith says, "No, my covenant God; Thou deservest something else. Thy honor requires that my children will praise and magnify Thee forever." The honor of God is worth so much to us that nothing seems to be more dishonoring than that our children, who bear the Name of the triune God on their foreheads, would curse and blaspheme God for-

ever. Thus the prayer of the congregation ends in the honor of
God. Her greatest pleading ground is that the Lord will be glorified in her children.

Therefore, the prayer of the congregation mirrors the promise of God. His promise was that He would glorify Himself in
her seed, and her prayer is that He will indeed do so. When
God's promise and our desire meet each other in truth, faith
says, "We thank and praise thee, that thou hast forgiven us, and
our children, all our sins, through the blood of thy beloved Son
Jesus Christ and hast adopted us to be thy children." It will all
end in the honor of God.

The administration of the covenant applies to many who
are not included in the covenant in truth. Many show through
their walk of life that they will have nothing to do with God's
covenant. Yet, the Lord will receive His honor even though they
reject the covenant offered to them. Even though the majority of
Israel turned away from the God of the covenant, and even
though the majority of the visible church does not esteem it
either, yet the administration of that covenant will bring about
the honor of God. God will fulfill His purpose with the preaching of the gospel, and His purpose is to gather a congregation of
elect sinners in the unity of true saving faith. Although an over-
whelming majority rejects this preaching, God will not be
hindered in fulfilling His purpose.

So it is with the administration of God's covenant in the
midst of the visible church. The end result will be what Paul
says in Romans 11:7: "But the election hath obtained it." Where
is boasting then? It is excluded. What will the end be? "Through
Thee alone, because of Thy eternal good pleasure."

CHAPTER 7

The Administration of Baptism to Adult Persons

The form for the administration of baptism is divided into two parts. The first part deals with the administration of baptism to infants of believers, and the second part deals with the administration of baptism to adults. Although the doctrinal part of the form is the same for both, the ground for the administration of baptism to an adult differs from that of infants of believers.

The form therefore reads, "However children of Christian parents (although they understand not this mystery) must be baptized by virtue of the covenant; yet it is not lawful to baptize those who are come to years of discretion, except they first be sensible of their sins, and make confession both of their repentance and faith in Christ." The subjects of baptism are different, and, therefore, there are differences in the forms for infants of believers and for adults. Infant baptism is grounded in the covenant of grace, which incorporates the children through their baptism with their parents. In contrast, adult baptism necessitates a personal faith in Christ. It is important to note this difference.

Adult persons may not be baptized unless they, sensible of their sins, do confession of their faith in Christ. The authors of the form base this on the Holy Scriptures:

> For this cause did not only John the Baptist preach (according to the command of God) the baptism of repentance, and

baptized, for the remission of sins, those who confessed their sins (Mark 1 and Luke 3); but our Lord Jesus Christ also commanded his disciples to teach all nations, and then to baptize them, in the name of the Father, and of the Son, and of the Holy Ghost (Matt. 28, Mark 16), adding this promise: "He that believeth and is baptized shall be saved." According to which rule, the Apostles, as appeareth from Acts 2, 10 and 16, baptized none who were of years of discretion, but such as made confession of their faith and repentance. Therefore it is not lawful now to baptize any other adult person, than such as have been taught the mysteries of holy baptism, by the preaching of the gospel, and are able to give an account of their faith by the confession of their mouth.

The Conditions for the Administration of Baptism to Adult Persons

The requirements for adult baptism differ from infant baptism. The proofs given by the form are abundantly clear. John the Baptist did not baptize everyone who came to him; he demanded a confession of sin and repentance. Only those who sorrowfully confessed their sin and who in faith looked for the Messiah to come were baptized. Baptism and confession of sin went together.

We observe the same thing on the day of Pentecost. Not everyone was baptized in the name of the Lord Jesus for the remission of sins, but only those who gladly received Peter's word. The eunuch was only baptized after he professed his personal faith in Christ. Time and again, when the New Testament speaks about baptism, it associates baptism with a confession of sin and faith in the Lord Jesus Christ. The apostles did not know the hearts of those they baptized, as evidenced by the baptism of Simon the sorcerer, but they did insist on a personal confession of sin and faith in Jesus Christ before they baptized anyone. Simon the sorcerer's baptism was based on his personal profession of faith in Christ as the only Savior and only later did it appear that it was not a true profession coming from the heart.

Thus, the apostles did not judge the heart, but they did demand a testimony of personal faith before they baptized an adult.

When the men of the Reformation drafted the form for the administration of adult baptism, they incorporated these biblical facts in the form: first a profession of a personal faith, then the administration of baptism as a means of incorporating into the Christian church, and finally the partaking of the Holy Supper. This is clear from the introduction and also from the questions that follow.

The Origin of the Form for the Administration of Adult Baptism

In the Netherlands, there was already need of a form for the administration of adult baptism in the early days of the Reformation. In 1602, the synods of the provinces of North Holland and South Holland decided that a form was needed to administer adult baptism. One year later, a draft was presented to the synod of Den Briel. It was read and accepted, but at the same time it was decided to use this form only until the time that the National Synod would compile a form. Shortly after these synods drew up their form, they received a request from the province of Gelderland for a copy, which was followed by a request from the province of Friesland in 1606. This meant that this form was being used in many provinces. The province of Zeeland decided to create their own, and the synod of Veere decided to adapt the form for the administration of infant baptism and to make it suitable for the administration of adult baptism. This appeared in 1611 as the edition of the liturgy of Schilders in Middelburg. Clearly, the Dutch churches needed a form to be used for administering adult baptism.

Many Jews joined the Christian church. There were also Gentiles from overseas colonies who became Christians. Many others, because of the influence of the Anabaptists and Socinians, had not been baptized as infants. Everywhere, the church sessions were confronted with the difficulty of what to do with adults who had not been baptized. Unfortunately, the various forms the different synods used were quite different from each other. This situation lasted until the national Synod of Dordrecht in the years 1618-1619, where the form as we have it now was drafted.

It is noteworthy that the confession, which the person to be baptized was asked to make, was expanded. Where the form from Zeeland read, "...the person to be baptized has heard and believed the gospel...," the national synod changed this to read, "...except they first be sensible of their sins, and make confession both of their repentance and faith in Christ." It is further noteworthy that there are five questions, which must be answered with "Yes" five times. These five questions have been adopted from the form of South Holland.

The Questions

Some people have said that the questions are too detailed. The first question concerns the trinity, the third with the deity of Christ. The fourth question asks the person to assent to all the articles of the Christian faith, while in the first three questions he already has been asked whether he believes in the trinity, and whether he believes the doctrines of creation, providence, inherited sin, and the incarnation of the Son of God. Some thought that question four was unnecessarily repetitive of the first three questions and could be omitted when one simple question could require their assent to all of the twelve articles of faith.

I cannot agree with this criticism. I believe that there are good reasons for asking five detailed questions. We must remember that adult baptisms concerned people who came from Jewish, Gentile, Socinian, or Anabaptist backgrounds. These questions are very meaningful to the Gentile, the Jew, and any other unbaptized person. And when we consider the questions, we notice a certain order.

The first question concerns the belief in the only true God, as He has revealed Himself in His Word. Through grace, a Christian comes to believe that the God of the Bible is the only and true God, Creator of heaven and earth. This is a big step to take for both Gentiles and Jews. For the Jew, faith in the triune God is particularly important. Considering this, it is appropriate to first ask whether one believes in the only true God, who is distinct in three Persons, and is the Creator and Keeper of all things.

The second question focuses on confessing that we are "conceived and born in sin, and wholly incapable of doing any good." This is connected with the confession "that thou hast frequently, in thought, word and deed, transgressed the commandments of the Lord: and whether thou art heartily sorry for these sins." This goes quite a bit deeper than simply an assent to the twelve articles of faith. A personal confession of guilt is demanded. The person who has learned the work of the Holy Spirit in the conviction of sin will heartily agree with it. It is very humbling to answer "Yes" to this question, but it is also necessary. How could anyone understand the mystery of baptism without this heartfelt sorrow for sin?

The third question deals with the great mystery of Christendom: "that Christ, who is true and eternal God, and very man, who took his human nature on him out of the flesh and blood of the virgin Mary, is given thee of God, to be thy Savior." Would it be right if the church did not ask for assent to this truth? This is the turning point in conversion. We learn to look to Christ and believe in Him as the incarnate Son of God.

Then it is asked: "and that thou dost receive by this faith, remission of sins in his blood." Baptism is a seal of God's promises of forgiveness of sins in the blood of Christ. That is the essence of baptism, and particularly so when an adult is baptized. The promises of the gospel that whosoever looks to the crucified Christ and believes in Him shall not perish, but have eternal life, are sealed in baptism. The converted adult rests on these promises through faith, not through the administration of baptism. It is right to emphasize this. Baptism does not perform some automatic work or miracle. Salvation is proclaimed to them who believe and this salvation must be believed and embraced through faith. Faith and baptism belong together and therefore we conclude that it is proper that the third question asks for faith.

The confession "that thou art made by the power of the Holy Ghost, a member of Jesus Christ and his Church" has a special meaning for an unbaptized adult. Unbaptized, he stands outside the church of God. Through baptism and faith in Christ, he may now become a member of Christ's church on earth. He is no longer a stranger and foreigner, but a fellow citizen with the saints, and of the household of God.

The fourth question relates to all the articles of the Christian faith and to true doctrine. Likewise, it concerns experiential knowledge of the Christian doctrine. The adult who is baptized also promises to "persevere in the use of the Lord's Supper." The promise to take part in the Lord's Supper has stirred up much discussion because people did not want to or dare to promise what the form required of them. The problem is still current today and many synods have discussed the issue. At first, they were unsure what to do. The Synod of South Holland decided to baptize those adults of whom they had good hope, even if they did not want to promise to partake of the Lord's Supper. The Synod of Friesland decided not to baptize adults who could not promise to attend the Lord's Supper. The church looked for an answer. It is noteworthy that the Reformed ministers felt inclined not to baptize if the person did not want to promise to attend the Lord's Supper, whereas the Remonstrants did not want to make this demand of the person. The Remonstrant convention of Utrecht (1612) decided that it was not necessary to promise to come to the Lord's Supper before one could be baptized as an adult.

We should not weaken this demand. The National Synod of Dordrecht brought unity into the Reformed Church. We find their conclusion of this discussion in the church order. Article 59 says, "Adults are through baptism incorporated into the Christian church, and are accepted as members of the church, and are therefore obliged also to partake of the Lord's Supper, which they shall promise to do at their baptism."

There was also some difference of opinion about the word "adult." The word adult signifies a person who has come to the years of discretion. But where should the line be drawn? When does one become an adult? This issue has been discussed in great detail at various ecclesiastical meetings; in the end, they agreed on the age of fourteen years. Infant baptism can no longer be administered to someone older than fourteen; adult baptism must then be administered. In accord with Scripture, the order to be followed with adults was first a confession of faith, and then the administration of baptism followed by partaking of the Lord's Supper.

The question remained whether such a person had to promise to partake of the Lord's Supper. Quite often the person concerned did desire to be baptized, but did not want to promise to partake of the Lord's Supper. Sometimes it was the other way round. The person did desire to promise to partake of the Lord's Supper after being baptized, but the church was of the opinion that the person to be baptized had received little instruction in the doctrine of the truth, and did not show any fruits of faith in his life. The church was reluctant to baptize in such cases.

Various synods discussed this issue, but the general feeling was that anyone who was baptized as an adult should come to the Lord's Supper. This issue was then dealt with by the National Synod of 1618-1619 who laid the matter to rest and decided that adult baptism must be connected with the use of the Lord's Supper. Hence the existence of article 59 in the Church Order. This obligation was then incorporated in the fourth baptismal question and the person to be baptized was to be asked to promise that he would attend the Lord's Supper in the presence of God.

The fifth question regards a firm resolution to walk in the way of the commandments of God. There must be a sincere desire to serve God and to obey His law.

A Matter of Deep Significance

By coming to a decisive conclusion and writing the form accordingly, the Synod of Dordrecht removed all uncertainty about whether someone baptized as an adult had to promise to use the Lord's Supper. It was their opinion that if someone's confession of faith and walk of life were not sufficient to allow him to come to the Lord's Supper, then he also should not be baptized.

When we read the introduction of the form for the administration of baptism to adults, we can understand why they came to this conclusion. They felt that to celebrate the Lord's Supper acceptably, we must have a true knowledge of our misery, a godly sorrow over sin, and a true faith in Jesus Christ. The same things are required for the administration of adult baptism, so the person who meets the requirements for adult baptism also meets the requirements for partaking of the Lord's Supper, and should promise to do so. In this light, we must understand the statement: "It is not lawful to baptize those who are come to the years of discretion, except they first be sensible of their sins, and make confession of their repentance and faith in Christ." This makes adult baptism an event of great significance. How necessary is proper self-examination here! An adult being baptized does not make confession of sin and faith before man, but before an all-knowing God. How do I know that my sorrow over sin and faith in Christ are the true work of the Holy Spirit? Important questions have to be considered.

I think that every unbaptized person who has been taught the truth has to consider first and foremost what being baptized does not mean. An unbaptized person stands outside of God's covenant and does not belong to the congregation of Christ, to which God gave His covenant promises. Our fathers of the Synod of Dordrecht strongly emphasized this in the discussion regarding article 70, which concerns marriage. They said that a marriage with an unbaptized person should not be confirmed in the church[5] because an unbaptized person is a heathen.

These are harsh and unpleasant things, but I do not think an unbaptized person can truly desire to be baptized without first knowing and experiencing them. The real issue is not who I

---

[5] Note that in the Netherlands, a couple marries *according to the law* in a municipal hall. Following this marriage ceremony, Protestant couples usually ask *God's blessing over their marriage* in a special church service. The Synod's comments refer to the church service only.

may marry but that being unbaptized means I stand outside of God's covenant and His promises, which He gave to His church. This is the issue that should affect us the most. The Holy Spirit must teach us what it means to stand outside the covenant, to be unconverted, to be without God in the world, to be without Christ on earth, and to be a stranger to the promises of the gospel. To really miss these things must make us want to be baptized. Therefore, I would like to say to all young adults who are unbaptized and who have come to know the truth and want to join the Christian church, "First think about what it means to be an unbaptized person!" When we read the form for the administration to adults earnestly and thoroughly, the biggest question should be, "Can I, and may I, answer these questions?"

A Personal Confession

We cannot pass by the questions in a light-hearted manner. I know that this has happened with many people, and it still happens today. Some say, "If you are sincere, you may desire baptism, even though you cannot say that you are converted." Others say, "You do not have to fulfill the promise to attend the Lord's Supper immediately. Simply pray that God will open a way for you some time in the future."

I do not believe that this is the solution. This may produce a certain degree of indifference, or the person concerned will have a lifelong problem with his conscience and ask himself continually, "Was it right to be baptized? I promised something I do not fulfill." These considerations should bring us on our knees to seek and to find a solution, imploring it from the Lord at the throne of His grace.

Even when, through God's grace, we repent of our sins and with a contrite heart believe in Christ as the only Savior, we may still struggle with the question, "Can I, and may I, answer these questions?"

It seems as though the questions speak of an assured faith. That is why the third question asks: "Dost thou believe that Christ, who is the true and eternal God, and very man, who took his human nature on him out of the flesh and blood of the

Virgin Mary, is given thee of God, to be thy Saviour, and that thou dost receive by this faith, remission of sins in his blood, and that thou art made by the power of the Holy Ghost, a member of Jesus Christ and his Church?"

In truth, this is a soul-searching question. This question does not just concern whether we are sorrowful over our sins, whether we look to Jesus, and whether we desire to walk in the ways of the Lord. The question asks for a very personal faith in Christ, which appropriates Christ as our personal Surety and Savior.

I believe that it was intentional to make this question so personal. Those who desire to be baptized must feel that they need a personal faith in Christ. On the other hand, we must consider the foundation for this personal faith. The word "given" used here means "given in the promises of the gospel." It concerns the kind of faith with which the guilty and lost sinner embraces Christ, who is offered in the gospel. We must realize that, although there is much doubting and struggling in the heart of a believer, this is not so in faith itself. Faith embraces the promise of God, in which God grants Christ and all His benefits to a poor sinner.

When this question is understood in this manner, we realize that it is not asking for an assured faith, but for a true faith in which certainty is always present. True faith embraces and appropriates. Although there are degrees in this appropriation, yet in every exercise of faith there is this appropriating and embracing. Nevertheless, it should bring us at the Lord's feet and make us seek for His confirmation.

I would advise those who struggle with this question not to read this question incorrectly. When we look at ourselves, there are a thousand barriers, and salvation is never possible. Who can answer five times with "Yes" to such significant questions? However, when by faith we look to the blood of Christ, we have no such hindrances. Rather, we hear, "Even if you had all the sins of Adam's posterity combined, the blood of Jesus cleanses you from all of them." To be baptized in this manner is what I heartily wish for all who seek to be baptized as an adult.

CHAPTER 8

Rebaptism

Many people reject infant baptism because their own baptism means nothing to them. They are looking for a new spiritual experience and think they can find it by being rebaptized as an adult. Such lack of respect for infant baptism is largely due to the influence of various Pentecostal groups. These groups strongly emphasize the work and gifts of the Spirit. Furthermore, "baptism by the Spirit" has greater importance than any other baptism.

These groups criticize the orthodox churches for missing the power of the Spirit and being dead institutions. Part of this criticism is directed at infant baptism, which they believe is not true baptism. Baptism is something that must be experienced; one must be baptized as a believer and not as an ignorant child. To them, baptism means a personal choice of faith and a conscious following of Christ into death, afterward to be resurrected with Him. Infant baptism is therefore seen as an ecclesiastical evil and a religion of outward form where the Spirit and His power are lacking. Adult baptism and baptism by the Spirit are *the* important issues in the Christian life.

This criticism has penetrated the orthodox churches and many people are open to it. A new spiritual impulse is sought, and thought to be found in rebaptism by immersion; only then do people consider themselves to be finally baptized in truth. By rebaptism, the relationship between faith and baptism—which, in their opinion, has been lost by the church—is restored.

We have to admit that this thinking is a reaction to superficial spiritual life, both in the church and in individuals. The church often no longer understands the power and meaning of infant baptism. Infant baptism has become a hollow ceremony, a custom, and nothing more. This is closely related to hollow Christianity in churchgoers. Where spiritual life is declining or has disappeared altogether, you will always find a superficial view of infant baptism. The church gives the impression that baptism has little meaning; baptism is only a ceremony without significance.

We find a striking similarity in the lack of appreciation regarding circumcision among the Israelites. When the life of faith among the Israelites became superficial and was only an outward performance (or lack of performing) certain duties, circumcision lost its power and meaning. Israel lost sight of the covenant of God and neglected the sign of this covenant. And this is the sad situation of the church today. We have lost sight of the covenant of grace and therefore of the sign of the covenant of God. Baptism has become simply an outward ceremony and custom.

As a reaction to this, many fall under the spell of adult rebaptism and the spectacular salvation supposedly connected with it. The spiritual enthusiasm of many of these groups is contagious and sparkles in comparison with the seemingly dull and declining orthodox church.

The church must admit its guilt in losing many members to such groups. It is true that modern man seeks some spiritual high, and thinks he can find it through adult rebaptism and baptism by the Spirit. Nevertheless, the orthodox church is also guilty. We have allowed infant baptism to lose its power and meaning through two errors.

First, the church has strongly overvalued infant baptism. Many churches have taught for many years that being baptized means you are a child of God. The doctrine of this optimistic view of the covenant was that all baptized children were regenerated until it was shown that the contrary was true. The necessity of a personal faith and repentance was not preached anymore. Baptism became the rock on which parents and children alike rested. The church became cold and dead despite all kinds of inventions to decorate the dead life of the church. Repentance and faith no longer functioned as they ought to have, and the life of faith disappeared from the church. What remained was merely a dead form.

Secondly, some churches strongly undervalued infant baptism. As a reaction to the false doctrine of baptismal regeneration, they taught that baptism was nothing more than an outward sign. It no longer demanded or promised anything. Many parents in orthodox churches do not understand why they have their children baptized or what baptism really means for them and their children. Likewise, the church no longer understands the power and the meaning of infant baptism.

Some people react to this by taking refuge in adult rebaptism. They think that this adult rebaptism has meaning for them and that it promises something to them. They expect that rebaptism will give them the experience of salvation in Christ. But what a mistake to take refuge in an outward ceremony such as adult rebaptism, and not in the God of our baptism, who sealed to our foreheads that the blood of Jesus Christ cleanses from all sin! When we seek our salvation in adult baptism, there is a danger that we deceive ourselves with mere enthusiasm, rather than exercising genuine faith.

Rebaptism does not bring us closer to the salvation of the Lord. It does not make us a better Christian. And, although the church may be guilty of promoting an outward and hollow view of infant baptism, this does not mean that the infant baptism administered in her midst is invalid. The way out of the problem is not rebaptism, but only by a true experience of infant baptism. The salvation signified and sealed by infant baptism must be sought after and experienced. Assurance and comfort will not be found by taking refuge in rebaptism, but only by fleeing to the God of your infant baptism as a guilty and penitent sinner.

Faith and Baptism

Supporters of adult rebaptism always emphasize that baptism and faith belong together. Their main objections against infant baptism are that there is no command found in Scripture to baptize children and that children do not understand the meaning of their baptism. Furthermore, their strongest proof of the legitimacy of adult baptism is that those who are baptized must believe. Thus, people who reject infant baptism point to Mark 16:16: "He that believeth and is baptized shall be saved." The order is clear: first faith, and then baptism.

These people also point to the circumcision of Abraham and say that according to Romans 4:11, Abraham first believed and then was circumcised: "And he received the sign of circumcision, a seal of the righteousness of the faith." The order was again first faith, and then circumcision.

We must immediately point out that this was indeed the case with Abraham, but not with the children of Abraham and the children of his servants. The order—first faith, then baptism—applies only to the unbaptized adult. Those who demand that no one may be baptized who does not believe exclude children from God's covenant. Calvin reminds such people of the saying, "He who will not work, shall not eat." He then says to these people that they would feed their children even if these children did not work, wouldn't they?

Faith followed by baptism is the order that applies in mission work. The apostles were not allowed to begin by administering baptism, but they had to begin by preaching. When faith grew as a result of preaching, then baptism was administered. Mark 16:16 concerns the baptism of adults who have come to faith; their children were baptized with them because they were included in the parents. In the book of Acts, we read of entire families being baptized. Think of the jailer and his house, of Lydia, and the household of Stephanas. The covenant of grace in the New Testament still applies to children. God maintains His promise: "I shall be a God unto thee, and to thy seed after thee in their generations." He promises to bestow His blessing on the children of the visible church (Isa. 44:3).

Additionally, faith, even the faith of an adult, can never be the essence of baptism. It is a fundamental error to make faith the ground of baptism. The crucial point is not the personal choice in faith to become the property of Christ; this can never be the essence of baptism. Paul does not say that circumcision was a seal of Abraham's faith, but of the righteousness of faith. Circumcision did not seal Abraham's faith, but the righteousness of Christ, on which the faith of Abraham relied. It sealed that he was a partaker of Christ's righteousness by faith in the promise of God. Circumcision and baptism point to the same issue, and are the signs and seals of the same salvation— namely, salvation through the righteousness of Christ. Faith is essential for salvation, but it is not the essence of circumcision or baptism. Circumcision and baptism do not point us to faith, but to Christ. They are sacraments that strengthen faith in Christ. Baptism is not a seal of inwardly experienced faith, but of the salvation in Christ promised by God.

It is true that the baptized child must experience the essence of baptism through faith. But, for children, baptism is a sign and seal of God's covenant. For the adult, who as a penitent sinner looks upon Christ, baptism is the seal of the salvation to which faith is directed—namely, salvation in Christ. The sacraments are not signs that seal our faith. They are seals attached to God's promises. We must be warned against making our personal choice, made in faith, the essence of and ground for baptism.

Without faith, we will not receive any benefit from the sacraments. All the blessings of God's covenant are obtained in the way of repentance and faith only. He who forgets this makes baptism a pillow to sleep on and promotes a false rest in the outward administration of baptism. But faith does not seal baptism. The focus must be on salvation in Christ. Therefore, Philip required of the eunuch that he believed in Christ before he was baptized (Acts 8:37). When we lose sight of God's covenant, we lose sight of the meaning of infant baptism.

The practice of rebaptism or a double baptism must therefore be rejected. Baptism is a sacrament of birth and cannot be repeated. We give assent to the covenant of God and receive the benefits of baptism only through repentance and faith.

Conclusion

I see no need to further engage in a detailed defense of infant baptism in this book. However, I do want to emphasize that, although our children may and must be baptized based on God's covenant, they still have to experience their baptism through faith when they grow up. They do not need a second baptism, but they do need to experience their baptism! Calvin points this out also and says, "We acknowledge, therefore, that at that time baptism profited us nothing, since in us the offered promise, without which baptism is nothing, lays neglected. Now, when by the grace of God we begin to repent, we accuse our blindness and hardness of heart in having been so long ungrateful for His great goodness" (*Institutes*, 4.15.17).

APPENDIX A

Form for the Administration of Baptism

The principal parts of the doctrine of holy baptism are these three:

First. That we with our children are conceived and born in sin, and therefore are children of wrath, insomuch that we cannot enter into the kingdom of God except we are born again. This, the dipping in, or sprinkling with water teaches us whereby the impurity of our souls is signified, and we admonished to loathe and humble ourselves before God, and seek for our purification and salvation without ourselves.

Secondly. Holy baptism witnesseth and sealeth unto us the washing away of our sins through Jesus Christ. Therefore we are baptized in the name of the Father, and of the Son, and of the Holy Ghost. For when we are baptized in the name of the Father, God the Father witnesseth and sealeth unto us, that he doth make an eternal covenant of grace with us, and adopts us for his children and heirs, and therefore will provide us with every good thing, and avert all evil or turn it to our profit. And when we are baptized in the name of the Son, the Son sealeth unto us, that he doth wash us in his blood from all our sins, incorporating us into the fellowship of his death and resurrection, so that we are freed from all our sins and accounted righteous before God. In like manner, when we are baptized in the name of the Holy Ghost, the Holy Ghost assures us, by this holy sacrament, that he will dwell in us and sanctify us to be members of Christ, applying unto us that which we have in Christ, namely, the washing away of our sins, and the daily renewing of our lives, till we shall finally be presented without spot or wrinkle among the assembly of the elect in life eternal.

Thirdly. Whereas in all covenants, there are contained two parts, therefore are we by God through baptism, admonished of, and obliged unto new obedience, namely, that we cleave to this one God, Father, Son, and Holy Ghost; that we trust in him, and love him with all our hearts, with all our souls, with all our mind, and with all our strength; that we forsake the world, crucify our old nature, and walk in a new and holy life.

And if we sometimes through weakness fall into sin, we must not therefore despair of God's mercy, nor continue in sin, since baptism is a seal and undoubted testimony that we have an eternal covenant of grace with God.

I. To Infants of Believers

And although our young children do not understand these things, we may not therefore exclude them from baptism, for as they are without their knowledge partakers of the condemnation in Adam, so are they again received unto grace in Christ; as God speaketh unto Abraham, the father of all the faithful, and therefore unto us and our children, saying, "I will establish my covenant between me and thee, and thy seed after thee, in their generations, for an everlasting covenant; to be a God unto thee, and to thy seed after thee" (Gen. 17:7). This also the apostle Peter testifieth, with these words, "For the promise is unto you and to your children, and to all that are afar off, even as many as the Lord our God shall call" (Acts 2:39). Therefore God formerly commanded them to be circumcised, which was a seal of the covenant, and of the righteousness of faith; and therefore Christ also embraced them, laid his hands upon them and blessed them (Mark 10).

Since then baptism is come in the place of circumcision, therefore infants are to be baptized as heirs of the kingdom of God, and of his covenant. And parents are in duty bound, further to instruct their children herein, when they shall arrive to years of discretion.

That therefore this holy ordinance of God may be administered to his glory, to our comfort, and to the edification of his Church, let us call upon his holy Name.

Prayer

Oh Almighty and eternal God, thou, who hast according to thy severe judgment punished the unbelieving and unrepentant world with the flood, and hast according to thy great mercy saved and protected believing Noah and his family; thou, who hast drowned the obstinate Pharaoh and his host in the Red Sea, and hast led thy people Israel through the midst of the Sea upon dry ground, by which baptism was signified—we beseech thee, that thou wilt be pleased of thine infinite mercy, graciously to look upon these children, and incorporate them by thy Holy Spirit into thy Son Jesus Christ, that they may be buried with him into his death, and be raised with him in newness of life; that they may daily follow him, joyfully bearing their cross, and cleave unto him in true faith, firm hope, and ardent love; that they may, with a comfortable sense of thy favor, leave this life, which is nothing but a continual death, and at the last day may appear without terror before the judgment seat of Christ thy Son, through Jesus Christ our Lord, who with thee and the Holy Ghost, one only God, lives and reigns forever. Amen.

An Exhortation to the Parents

Beloved in the Lord Jesus Christ, you have heard that baptism is an ordinance of God, to seal unto us and to our seed his covenant; therefore it must be used for that end, and not out of custom or superstition. That it may then be manifest that you are thus minded, you are to answer sincerely to these questions:

First. Whether you acknowledge, that although our children are conceived and born in sin, and therefore are subject to all miseries, yea, to condemnation itself; yet that they are sanctified[1] in Christ, and therefore, as members of his Church ought to be baptized?

Secondly. Whether you acknowledge the doctrine which is contained in the Old and New Testaments, and in the articles of the Christian faith, and which is taught here in this Christian Church, to be the true and perfect[2] doctrine of salvation?

Thirdly. Whether you promise and intend to see these children, when come to the years of discretion (whereof you are either parent or witness), instructed and brought up in the aforesaid doctrine, or help or cause them to be instructed therein, to the utmost of your power?

Answer. Yes.

Then the Minister of God's Word, in baptizing, shall say, N., I baptize thee in the name of the Father, and of the Son, and of the Holy Ghost. Amen.

Thanksgiving

Almighty God and merciful Father, we thank and praise thee that thou hast forgiven us and our children all our sins, through the blood of thy beloved Son Jesus Christ, and received us through thy Holy Spirit as members of thine only begotten Son, and adopted us to be thy children, and sealed and confirmed the same unto us by holy baptism; we beseech thee, through the same Son of thy love, that thou wilt be pleased always to govern these baptized childen by thy Holy Spirit, that they may be piously and religiously educated, increase and grow up in the Lord Jesus Christ, that they then may acknowledge thy fatherly goodness and mercy, which thou hast shown to them and us, and live in all righteousness under our only Teacher, King and High Priest, Jesus Christ; and manfully fight against, and overcome sin, the devil and his whole dominion, to the end that they may eternally praise and magnify thee, and thy Son Jesus Christ, together with the Holy Ghost, the one only true God. Amen.

II. To Adult Persons

However children of Christian parents (although they understand not this mystery) must be baptized by virtue of the covenant, yet it is not lawful to baptize those who are come to years of discretion, except they first be sensible of their sins, and make confession both of their repentance and faith in Christ. For this cause did not only John the Baptist preach (according to the command of God) the baptism of repentance, and baptized, for the remission of sins, those who confessed their sins (Mark 1 and Luke 3); but our Lord Jesus Christ also commanded his disciples to teach all nations, and then to baptize them, in the name of the

Father, and of the Son, and of the Holy Ghost (Matt. 28; Mark 16), adding this promise: "He that believeth and is baptized shall be saved." According to which rule, the Apostles, as appeareth from Acts 2, 10 and 16, baptized none who were of years of discretion, but such as made confession of their faith and repentance. Therefore it is not lawful now to baptize any other adult person, than such as have been taught the mysteries of holy baptism, by the preaching of the gospel, and are able to give an account of their faith by the confession of the mouth.

That therefore this holy ordinance of God may be administered to his glory, to our comfort, and to the edification of his Church, let us call upon his holy name:

Oh Almighty and eternal God, thou, who hast according to thy severe judgment punished the unbelieving and unrepentant world with the flood, and hast according to thy great mercy saved and protected believing Noah and his family; thou, who hast drowned the obstinate Pharaoh and his host in the Red Sea, and hast led thy people Israel through the midst of the Sea upon dry ground, by which baptism is signified—we beseech thee, that thou wilt be pleased of thine infinite mercy, graciously to look upon this person, and incorporate him by thy Holy Spirit into thy Son Jesus Christ, that he may be buried with him into his death, and be raised with him in newness of life, that he may daily follow him, joyfully bearing his cross, and cleave unto him in true faith, firm hope, and ardent love; that he may with a comfortable sense of thy favor, leave this life, which is nothing but a continual death, and at the last day, may appear without terror before the judgment seat of Christ thy Son, through Jesus Christ our Lord, who with thee and the Holy Ghost, one only God, lives and reigns forever. Amen.

Since therefore thou, N., art also desirous of holy baptism, to the end that it may be to thee a seal of thine ingrafting into the Church of God; that it may appear that thou dost not only receive the Christian religion, in which thou hast been privately instructed by us and of which also thou hast made confession before us, but that thou (through the grace of God) intendest and purposest to lead a life according to the same, thou art sincerely to give answer before God and his Church.

First. Dost thou believe in the only true God, distinct in three persons, Father, Son, and Holy Ghost, who has made heaven and earth, and all that in them is, of nothing, and still maintains and governs them, insomuch that nothing comes to pass, either in heaven or on earth, without his divine will?

Answer. Yes.

Secondly. Dost thou believe that thou art conceived and born in sin, and therefore art a child of wrath by nature, wholly incapable of doing any good, and prone to all evil; and that thou hast frequently, in thought, word and deed, transgressed the commandments of the Lord; and whether thou art heartily sorry for these sins?

Answer. Yes.

Thirdly. Dost thou believe that Christ, who is the true and eternal God, and very man, who took his human nature on him out of the flesh and blood of the Virgin Mary, is given thee of God, to be thy Savior, and that thou dost receive by this faith, remission of sins in his blood, and that thou art made by the power of the Holy Ghost, a member of Jesus Christ and his Church?

Answer. Yes.

Fourthly. Dost thou assent to all the articles of the Christian religion, as they are taught here in this Christian Church, according to the Word of God; and purpose steadfastly to continue in the same doctrine to the end of thy life; and also dost thou reject all heresies and schisms repugnant to this doctrine, and promise to persevere in the communion of the Christian Church, not only in the hearing of the Word, but also in the use of the Lord's Supper?

Answer. Yes.

Fifthly. Hast thou taken a firm resolution always to lead a Christian life; to forsake the world and its evil lusts, as is becoming the members of Christ and his Church; and to submit thyself to all Christian admonitions?

Answer. Yes.

The good and great God mercifully grant his grace and blessing to this thy purpose, through Jesus Christ. Amen.

Thanksgiving
Almighty God and merciful Father, we thank and praise thee that thou hast forgiven us and our children all our sins, through the blood of thy Son Jesus Christ, and received us through thy Holy Spirit as members of thine only begotten Son, and adopted us to be thy children, and sealed and confirmed the same unto us by holy baptism. We beseech thee, through the same Son of thy love, that thou wilt be pleased always to govern this baptized person by thy Holy Spirit, that he may lead a Christian and godly life, and increase and grow up in the Lord Jesus Christ, that he may acknowledge thy fatherly goodness and mercy, which thou hast shown to him and to us, and live in all righteousness, under our only Teacher, King, and High Priest, Jesus Christ; and that he may manfully fight against and overcome sin, the devil and his whole dominion, to the end that he may eternally praise and magnify thee, and thy Son Jesus Christ, together with the Holy Ghost, the one only true God. Amen.

---

[1] "My children" (Ezek. 16:21). They are holy (1 Cor. 7:14).

[2] Dutch, *volkomene*; English, complete.

Printed in the United States
57287LVS00003B/1-102